SULTAN RAZIYA

SULTANATE OF DELHI
IN
CIRCA 1235 A.D.

SULTAN RAZIYA

Her Life and Times: A Reappraisal

MANOHAR
2016

First published 1990
Reprinted 2016

ISBN 978-81-85425-09-2

Published by
Ajay Kumar Jain *for*
Manohar Publishers & Distributors
4753/23 Ansari Road, Daryaganj
New Delhi 110 002

Typest by
A J Software Publishing Co. Pvt. Ltd.
New Delhi 110 005

Printed at
Salasar Imaging Systems
Delhi 110 035

EXPLANATORY NOTE ON REFERENCES/ CHAPTERS

All references to Minhaj are from Minhaj-ud-din Siraj Jurjani *Tabaqat-i-Nasiri.*

English translation by Major H.G. Raverty—wherever the name of the editor/translator Raverty is mentioned it is in connection with his footnotes wherein he points out the contradictions/variations etc. and his own views of the various Mss of Minhaj's *Tabaqat-i-Nasiri* that he studied for the above translation. His comments have also taken into account the writings on later chroniclers.

References to later chroniclers such as Barani, Nizami, Ibn Batuta who have written about 13th century Muslim rulers of India have been taken from *The History of India as told by its own Historians* - The Muhammadan period edited from the posthumous papers of the late Sir H.M. Elliot, K.C.B. East India Company, Bengal Civil Service by Professor John Dowson, M.R.A.S. Staff College, Sandhurst, Vol. III, London, Trubner & Co., 1871 unless other translators' works are cited in the footnotes.

The chapter on Administrative, Legal and Economic set up uses a number of Turko-Persian titles given to functionaries of the State. These titles do not necessarily convey the literal meaning of the title. Therefore, these titles are explained by the functions performed by the title holders. Additionally, vernacular words, wherever considered important, have been explained in the glossary for the benefit for the reader.

THE TURKISH SULTANS OF DELHI

Qutb-ud-din Aibak	d. 1210
Aram Shah	d. 1211
Shams-ud-din Iltutmish	d. 1236
Rukn-ud-din Firuz Shah	d. 1236
Raziya	d. 1240
Muiz-ud-din Behram	d. 1242
Ala-ud-din Masud	deposed 1246
Nasir-ud-din Mahmud	d. 1266
Ghiyas-ud-din Balban	d. 1287
Muiz-ud-din Kaiqubad	d.1290

CONTENTS

PREFACE

Sultan Raziya, the only woman in India crowned as queen in her own right, had a brief though eventful reign. She was de jure the fifth muslim ruler of Delhi but de facto the third, two predecessors, one of them her brother, having been short-lived and not worthy of note.

For some reason, historians have by and large ignored this very important era of the beginning of muslim rule which started a new chapter in Indian history. Some good work has certainly been done but the writers have, as it were, drawn a tight curtain between invaders' incursion into India and the state of affairs in their own homeland. This has led to a very lopsided view of the history of the early muslim times in India leaving little scope for comparison of institutions and behavioural patterns on both sides of the border and, above all, allowing a great deal of distortion of facts. Thus, while we hear of Mahmud of Ghazni's merciless raids on Hindu temples we have never been allowed to have a glimpse of his Hindu soldiers desecreting mosques and churches in his co-religionist states at his orders. Similarly, very few students of Indian history have ever learnt about the burning of Ghazni by Ala-ud-Din of Ghur or even, on the Indian side, of the pillage of Indian temples by Hindus themselves.

Rich material is readily available to the student of medieval Indian history. Every ruler had his own chronicler and with all concessions made for exaggerations and hyperbole, the facts are, by and large, correctly recounted. The British rulers also did yeoman service by translating practically all the major works into English. Certain twists may have been given to produce desired political results but mostly the translations are authentic and well annotated.

Raziya's own historian, Minhaj-us-Siraj Jurjani, was a remarkable man and a good historian, although it must be admitted that he has not done justice to her. In a monumental work tracing the history of muslim kingdoms from the inception of the world according to Islam, up to the latter half of the 13th century A.D. he has devoted a total of only 12 pages to her reign. These in translation include Raverty's footnotes and annotations. The bare facts of her career as sovereign perhaps do not merit more space but, as in the case of other sovereigns, he could have enlivened the narrative with short anecdotes of her early life, of her appearance, of the martial games she obviously played in her youth and various aspects of her personality. However, he has done nothing of the kind, sternly sticking to a straight laced account of her 3 odd years of rule. Perhaps it was because of the constraint of writing about a woman and the fear of being accused of lack of respect towards her sex that he has written just what needed to be recounted and not a word more.

A modern historian, therefore, has no choice but to try to maximise this meagre material and place Raziya within the context of her times while examining her considerable contribution to the history of the age which was in no way hampered by her sex or by her supposed affair (the fabrication of later historians) with the Ethiopian, Yakut.

Minhaj's treatment of Raziya in no way detracts from his towering stature both as an ecclesiastic and chronicler. A scion of a family of distinguished scholars and ecclesiastics (his father was Qazi of the Ghurian troops stationed at Lahore) he was born in the same year in which Delhi was declared capital of the Turkish empire in India by Qutb-ud-Din Aibak who later became its first Sultan. He was decorated with honours by various monarchs and held many high posts such as Iman, Qazi and Khatib of Gwalior and Superintendent of the Nasiriah College at Delhi and later became Chief Qazi. He served all Sultans from Iltutmish to Nasir-ud-Din Mohammad Shah, Raziya's brother who succeeded her to throne, and after whom his book is named and so was a ringside witness to all the events of the period. He travelled widely, studying the history of and conditions in, the far-flung areas of the empire. All of these he has reported with meticulous care and largely unbiased objectivity, although always within the bounds of an Islamic framework.

The work has been translated from the original Persian manuscript by Major H.G. Raverty, another meticulous scholar. His annotations account for almost two-thirds of the translated volumes. Not only does he compare the various copies of the manuscript "Tabakat-i-Nasiri" and point out the discrepancies in them but also the discrepancies appearing in different parts of the same volume. He also takes facts, such as Raziya's supposed affair with Yakut and, with quotations from the respective authors, underscores later distortions and flights of fancy.

Minhaj himself took the administrative, financial and judicial set-up of his times for granted and concerned himself only with political events, but modern scholars like Habibullah, Muhammad Habib, K.A. Nizami, I.H. Qureshi and others have delved deeply into the matter and given a comprehensive view of the statecraft of the times.

The present work has drawn from all available sources and attempts to give a comprehensive view of the life and times of Sultan Raziya, and place her in proper niche in Indian history.

I am deeply indebted to Dr. Muzzafar Alam of Jawaharlal University of New Delhi for his valuable suggestions as well as providing the map of India showing extent of rule of the Sultanate period and invaluable assistance in providing English translation for the Glossary. Faults, if any, in the book are entirely mine.

Special thanks are due to Mr. J.L. Malhotra who has helped in the preparation of the text and to the librarians and library staff of the Indian Council for Cultural Relations and the Jamia Millia Islamia for their readiness in providing books and other help required.

1

ANTECEDENTS

The first Muslim dynasty to rule India has been variouly termed "Slave", "Pathan", "Afghan" and "Turko-Afghan". None of these titles is, however, correct. Though the first rulers had been slaves, they had all received letters of manumission before ascending the throne. It is also true that they came to India through Afghanistan which resulted in the nomenclature of Pathan, Afghan etc, but the fact remains that they were of pure Turkish origin and so, by right, that is what the true appellation of the dynasty should be.[1] The common Indian has always been aware of this and the generic term for all Muslims in India, for generations, was Turk.

Shihab-ud-Din Muiz-ud-Din Muhammad bin Sam, of the Shamsabaniah dynasty, known to countless generations of students of Indian history under British teachers, as Muhammad Ghori, actually came to India from Ghazni where he was installed as Sultan by his brother Ghiyas-ud-Din, ruler of Ghur, after his conquest of the area[2] in 1173.[3] He was not a great general and was more noted for his defeats than for his victories. The army of Ghazni, under his leadership, was badly defeated by the nobles of the area and would have been annihilated had not his brother, Ghiyas-ud-Din, come to his aid and turned the tide of the battle.[4] Muhammad Ghori was later defeated in India by the Rai of Nahrwalah, a brave young man with a large army of soldiers and elephants.[5] Later still, he was again defeated by Rai Pithora also known as Prithvi Raj Chauhan at Tarain, severely wounded in the arm by a javelin and forced to turn back to Ghazni.[6]

However, what he lacked in qualities of generalship he made up in persistence. After every defeat he marshalled his forces and returned to the fray to ultimate victory. When he returned to fight Rai Pithora one year later, the victory was his.

Battle of Tarain

Minhaj-us-Siraj recounts the story thus "The author heard from a trustworthy person, a distinguished man of the highland district of Tulak, whom they used to style by the title of Muinuddin Ushi, who said, "I was in that army with the Sultan-i-Ghazi and the number of cavalry composing the army of Islam that year was one hundred and twenty thousand arrayed in defensive armour. When the Sultan-i-Ghazi with such like organisation and such a force arrived near unto Rae Kolah Pithora, he had gained possession of the fortress of Tabarhindah by capitulation and had pitched his camp in the neighbourhood of Tarain (near Thanesar). The Sultan [now] made disposition of his forces. The centre division of the army, the baggage, the standards and banners, his canopy of State and the elephants, were left several miles in the rear. He marshalled his ranks and was advancing leisurely. The light-armed and uencumbered horsemen, he had directed should be divided into four divisions and had appointed them to act against the infidels on four sides; and the Sultan had commanded, saying; "It is necessary that on the right and left, and front and rear, 10,000 mounted archers should keep the infidel host in play; and when their elephants, horsemen, and foot advance to the attack, you are to face about and keep the distance of a horse's course in front of them". The musallman troops acted according to these instructions and having exhausted and wearied the unbelievers, Almighty God gave the victory to Islam and the infidel host was overthrown."

Rae Pithora, who was riding an elephant, dismounted and got upon a horse and fled [from the field], until in the neighbourhood of [the] Sursuti, he was taken prisoner and they despatched him to hell; and Gobind Rae of Dihli was slain in the engagement. The Sultan recognised his head through two teeth which had been broken [in the previous fighting]. The seat of government, Ajmir, with the whole of the Siwalikh [territory] such as Hansi, Surusti and other tracts, were subjugated. These events took place and this victory was achieved in 588 A.H. (1191 A.D.) and the Sultan placed Malik Kutb-ud-Din I-bak in the fort of Kuhram and thus returned home again." "Malik Kutb-ud-Din advanced from Kuhram to Mirath and took that city and fortress and, in the following year (1192 A.D.) he possessed himself of the capital city, Dihli."[7]

This decisive victory laid the foundation of the Sultanate of Delhi.

Earlier, in 1175 A.D. Shihabuddin having defeated his co-religionists, the Ismailis of Multan, had taken the fortress of Ucch. In 1179 he occupied Peshawar and established a fortress at Sialkot in 1181 A.D. Then, allying himself with Vijaya Dev, ruler of Jammu, he defeated Khusrau Malik, the last representative of the dynasty of Subuktagin and Mahmud of Ghazni, who had possession of Lahore.[8]

Contrary to popular belief, the early route into India from the Sulaiman mountains was neither through the Khyber nor the Bolan Pass. It was through the Gomal Pass which led to Dera Ismail Khan and thence to upper Sind Sagar Doab, through which the invaders entered the sub-continent. This is borne out by the fact that throughout the 12th and 13th centuries the first point of attack from beyond the Sulaiman Range was Ucch or Multan and not Lahore or Peshawar. The main battles were fought in the hundred mile gap between the Shivalik and Aravalli ranges in the plains extending from the Sutlej to the Jamuna. Once the invader entered the Gangetic plain, progress would become easy until he came to the eastern bend of the river against an entrance narrowed by the northern spheres of the Vindhya ranges and the Terai, the foothills of the Himalayas, after which they would follow the watercourses up to and into Bengal. Politically also the Khyber area was not safe, the tribes of the Sind Sagar Doab being perpetually hostile.[9] It was Upper Sind, therefore, that the founder of the Delhi Sultanate reached on his first expedition into India.

Muhammad's slave and trusted general Qutbuddin Aibak captured Hansi, Meerut, Delhi, Ranthambhor and Koil. In 1194 he helped his master defeat Jaichand, ruler of Benaras and Kannauj at Chandwar in Etawah district. In 1202 he captured the fortress of Kalinjar, and occupied Mahoba and Badaun.[10]

When Shihabuddin was assassinated on his way to Ghazni he left no male heirs to succeed. He had no sons and his daughter had died before him. It was therefore not posible to bring together the acquired and ancestral properties under one rule and his easy-going nephew Nasiruddin, in return for presents, gave *Khat-i-azadi*, (letters of manumission) to the three great slave officers of his uncle, i.e. Qutbuddin Aibak, Nasiruddin Qabacha and Taj-ud-din Yalduz and confined himself to his ancestral lands. By this act of manumission, he automatically set free all of Muhammad's slaves since without a master there can be no slave. The slaves thus became the co-heirs of the Sultan of Delhi and the throne could be occupied, through force or intrigue, only by those whom they supported or approved. The Sultan was thus not a supreme ruler, just prima inter pares, first among equals, holding office only if he kept his peers pleased.[11]

The provincial viceroys soon established their own authority in the areas which were under their jurisdiction. Thus Taj-ud-din Yalduz, Governor of Kirman, ascended the throne of Ghazni while Qutbuddin was declared ruler of the Indian territories. This excited the jealousy of Taj-ud-din Yalduz who endeavoured to conquer Punjab but was defeated by Qutbuddin and driven out of Ghazni. According to Minhaj "he (Qutbuddin) occupied the throne for a period of forty days and during this space of time, he was wholly engaged in revelry, and in bestowing largesse, and the affairs of the country, through this constant festivity were neglected."[12]

These events disgusted the inhabitants of the area who invited Yalduz to come to their rescue. Qutbuddin was driven out of Ghazni and returned to Delhi. This destroyed the chance of a political union between Ghazni and Delhi and Qutubuddin became a purely Indian Sultan.[13] His ascent to the throne was legalised by a canopy of State sent to him by Mahmud, Muhammad's nephew, who also bestowed on him the title of Sultan. In 602 A.H./1206 A.D. Qutbuddin proceeded from Delhi to Lahore and "on the 17th of the month, Zi-Kadah of the same year, he ascended the throne in the royal Kasr of Lahore.[14]

QUTBUDDIN AIBAK

Qutbuddin is described by Minhaj as being high spirited and open handed. In fact, his generosity was so great that the writer termed him a second Hatim. Raverty in a footnote to the text, comments that his liberality was so great that it became proverbial and Indians, when they wished to bestow the ultimate praise for generosity on a person, called him Qutbuddin-i-Kal, that is, the Qutbuddin of the age. He was also known as lakh-baksh, the bestower of lakhs, a title also bestowed on Rai Lakshmaniah of Bihar, his contemporary. The Sultan's "gifts" according to Minhaj, "were bestowed by hundreds of thousands, and his slaughters likewise were by hundreds of thousands."[15]

As a boy, Qutbuddin was captured by slave traders in Turkistan and brought to Nishapur where the Chief Kazi, a man of a renowned family, bought him and, says Minhaj, "in attendance on, and along with his sons, he read the word of God, and acquired instruction in horsemanship and shooting with the bow and arrow, so that in a short time, he became commented upon and favourably spoken of for his manly bearing." Apparently he was sold again, ". . . certain merchants brought him to Ghazni; and the Sultan-i-Ghazi, Muizuddin Muhammad, son of Sam, purchased him from those traders.''[16]

Apparently, though possessed of various endearing qualities and noted for his outstanding record as a soldier and administrator, Qutbuddin "possessed no outward comeliness and the little finger (of one hand) had a fracture and on that account he used to be styled I-bak-i-Shil (the powerless fingered).''[17]

It was his generosity that brought him to Muhammad's notice for, when, during a convivial party the Sultan bestowed lavish gifts of gold, silver and money on those present, Qutbuddin gave away everything he had received to his brother. Muhammad was very impressed and from then on, Qutbuddin rose steadily in rank and favour until he achieved the office of the Amir-i-Akhur (Lord of the Stables). Later he distinguished himself in various battles leading the armies that captured numerous Indian forts.

Qutbuddin also made matrimonial alliances with other Turkish Chiefs and potential rivals. He married Taj-ud-din Yalduz's daughter and married his sister to Nasir-ud-din Qabacha, another powerful rival. He gave his own daughter to Shamsuddin Iltutmish.[18]

In 607 A.H. (1210 A.D.) Qutbuddin fell from his horse while playing polo and the horse came down upon him "in such wise that the prominent part of the front of the saddle came upon his blessed chest and he died.''[19] He was buried at Lahore and for centuries his grave remained a place of pilgrimage although later, according to Raverty, the building was converted by the British into a library or a place of Chirstian worship.[20]

ARAM SHAH

The status of Aram Shah and his realtionship to Qutbuddin is vague. Some historians seem to think that he was the latter's son while Abul Fazl makes the statement that he was Qutbuddin's brother.[21] Minhaj states categorically that Qutbuddin had three daughters and fails to mention any son. He makes the bold statement that Aram Shah was raised to the throne without mentioning his lineage, nationality or even whether he was an adopted son. He goes on to say that "Qutbuddin contemplated Sultan Shamsuddin acquiring dominion, and he had called him son and had conferred on him the fief of Badaun.''[22]

Reverty states that the nobles and chieftains who were in Lahore at the time of Qutbuddin's death, set up Aram Baksh, adopted son of Qutbuddin on the throne in order to preserve tranquillity and gave him the title of Aram Shah. Mandates and decrees were issued in his name and "glad tidings of justice and impartiality towards the people" reached them (probably other nobles). This was, it is said, in 607 H."[23]

However, not everyone was pleased with the new ruler and Amir Ali-i-Ismaili, the *Sipah Salar*, and Governor of the city and province of Delhi got together with some other important officials and sent an invitation to Iltutmish to come to Delhi and take over the government. This, Iltutmish hastened to do along with a number of his followers.

In the meanwhile, Nasir-ud-din Qabacha, who had married two of Qutbuddin's daughters (one after the death of the other), appropriated Sind and Multan, Bhakar and Siwastan and, subsequently the Kuhram; the Khalji chiefs in Bengal declared their independence and the Hindu chiefs on the frontiers of the Muslim dominions became restless and rebellious.

Aram Shah, becoming aware of Iltutmish's occupation of Delhi, advanced with a strong force towards the city and the two armies confronted each other on the plain of Jud near Delhi.

However, Aram Shah was no match for the formidable Iltutmish and he was routed and disppeared, probably killed by his rival. Some historians assert that his reign was terminated within one year, but others state the length of the reign to have been 3 years. An inscription on a coin of Aram Shah and one of Iltutmish would seem to prove the latter to be correct. The first has the inscription "This diram (is) stamped with the name of the Malik, the shadow of the Almighty, in the year 607". On the reverse is stated "struck in the Dar-us-Sultanat, the city of Lahore." Iltutmish's coin says "612, the first of his reign."[24]

ILTUTMISH

Iltutmish belonged to the Ilbari tribe of Turkestan. His father, I-lam Khan, was a leader of his tribe who had a large family and numerous dependents and followers. As a boy, Iltutmish was known as Shamsud-din and became the envy of his brothers because of his good looks, intelligence and fine disposition which made him very popular with everyone. He was also called Iltutmish (the name is spelt differently by different authors, Raverty spelling it I-Yal-Timish) because he was born on a night during an eclipse of the moon, and this was the normal title given to a Turk born on such a night.[25]

Elliot spells the name as Altamsh, Elphinstone as Altamish, while Berthold suggested that the word was really Iltutmish, maintainer of the kingdom.[26] According to Md. Habib some verses of Amir Khusrau and Nizamuddin Auliya make it clear that the name Iltutmish was synonymous with Alamgir and Jahangir (world conqueror).[27]

Early Life

The brothers (or perhaps cousins) one day lured him away from the parental roof on the pretext of showing him a herd of horses, and then sold him to some merchants who brought him to Bukhara and sold him to a kinsman of the Sadr-i-Jahan (Chief ecclesiatic) of the city. Here he was brought up kindly and was treated as one of the children of the family.

Iltutmish himself is said to have recounted this stroy about himself: "On a certain occasion, one of the [above mentioned] family gave me a small piece of money saying, 'Go into the market and buy some grapes and bring them'. When I set out for the market, I lost, by the way, that bit of money; and through my youthful age, out of fear at what had happened I fell a crying. Whilst thus lamenting, I was joined by a good *Darwesh* who took me by the hand and purchased for me some grapes which he gave me and he made me promise (saying) 'when thou attainest unto power and dominion thou will ever regard devotees and ascetics with reverence, and watch over their weal'. I gave him my promise; and all the prosperity and blessings which I acquired have been through the compassionate regard of that *Darvesh.*"[28]

It was perhaps to this incident that Iltutmish's generosity, faith and reverence towards holy men can be ascribed.

Minhaj who so highly praised the bounteous generosity of Qutbuddin Aibak, puts his successor's largesse at a hundred times more. He writes "Towards men of various sorts and degrees, *Qazis, Imams, Muftis* and the like and to *darweshes* and monks, landowners and farmers, traders, strangers and travellers from great cities his benefactions were universal. Form the very outset of his reign and the dawn of the morning of his sovereignty, in the congregation of eminent doctors of religion and law, venerable *Saiyids, Maliks, Amirs, Sadrs* and [other] great men, the Sultan used yearly to expend about ten millions; and people from various parts of the world gathered together at the capital city of Dihli, which is the seat of government of Hindustan ..."[29]

Iltutmish was sold again to a merchant of Bukhara and then to another merchant styled, interestingly enough, Jamal-ud-Din Muhammad of the Tight Tunic, perhaps because of his girth which could not be easily contained within a garment. This time he was brought to Ghazni and so outstanding were his qualifications that he was recommended to Sultan Muizuddin himself. He, along with another Turk, I-bak, were in one team and the merchant was offered a sum of one thousand dinars of pure Rukni gold for the two but, considering the price too low, the merchant refused to sell. This incensed the Sultan who prohibited the sale of the two slaves in Ghazni. The merchant stayed in Ghazni for a year and then took the two young men with him to Bukhara where they stayed for three years. Still not finding anyone to meet his price he brought them back to Ghazni only to find that the prohibition against the sale continued. After one year, however, Qutbuddin Aibak visited Ghazni after his capture of Gujarat and pleaded with the Sultan to let him buy Iltutmish. The Sultan relented only to the point of saying, "Since a command has been issued that he should not be purchased at Ghazni, let them take him to the city of Dihli and there he can be purchased." The slaves were thus brought to Delhi where they were purchased for a sum of a hundred thousand jitals. Iltutmish was made Sadr-i-Jandars (Chief of the Jandars or guards) to Qutbuddin who called him his son and kept him at his side.

Promotions

Rising steadily in rank, becoming Amir-i-Shikar (Chief of the Hunt) and then Amir of Gwalior, Iltutmish acquired the fief town of Baran and its dependencies. His feats of valour, especially during an engagement with the Khokhar tribe when he rode into the river Jhelum in pursuit of the rebels and inflicted great casualties on them, caught the attention of Muizuddin Muhammad Ghuri who conferred on him a special dress of honour and issued a letter of manumission releasing him from slavery. He also told Qutbuddin Aibak "Treat Iltutmish well, for he will distinguish himself." [30]

The manumission was a signal honour, for up to that time senior slaves such as Aibak, Qabacha and Yalduz had not been manumitted. Now the Sultan had set free the slave of one of his own slaves. However, the matter seems to have been kept a secret since on his accession to the throne a deputation of the *ulema*, headed by *Qazi* Wajihuddin Kahani, waited on Iltutmish to find out if he had obtained a deed of manumission. He showed them the document and so was considered fit to become ruler.[31]

After his accession to the throne of Delhi in 1210 or 1211 Iltutmish faced the task of ousting his two main rivals Yalduz and Qabacha and keeping others in line. Around the coffin of Muhammad Ghuri, as it proceeded from Damyak, the place where he was assassinated, to Ghazni, a severe struggle broke out between the Ghurian officers and the Turkish slaves and the latter put Yalduz, the seniormost slave officer on the throne of Ghazni in 1206.[32]

Subsequently, Yalduz entered into an agreemant with and sent Iltutmish a Canopy of state and a *Durbash.*[33] The Durbash, literally meaning "Stand aside", was a kind of spear with two horns or branches ornamented with precious stones and gold and silver. This used to be carried in front of the sovereign when he went out so that people, seeing it, would know that the king was coming and move aside. It was also carried in battle so that if any one threw a lasso at the king the Durbash could help deflect the aim.[34]

Later, when Yalduz was dirven out of Ghazni by the Khwarinzmians he moved on to Lahore, which Qabacha had claimed as his own domain, ousted him and occupied it, extending his power beyond the city. Iltutmish knew that he must strike before his rival was firmly established in the Punjab otherwise he would not be safe in Delhi. He marched out to see for himself the extent of Yalduz's domain. The latter sent him a message claiming to be the rightful successor of Sultan Muizuddin Muhammad Ghuri and thus to have prior claim to the empire of Hindustan. To this, Iltutmish replied 'Times have changed. There is a new order now. What has happened to the Ghaznavids and the Ghurids? The times of hereditary descent are over." However, he offered to discuss the matter personally with Yalduz if both came unarmed and unaccompanied. Yalduz,however,decided to fight and was defeated in 1215-16 at the historic battlefield of Tarain where Muizuddin's victory had led to the establishment of kingdom of Hindustan. This meant not only the removal of a dangerous rival from Iltutmish's path but the final break with Ghazni, giving an independent status to the kingdom of Delhi.[35]

There was constant conflict between Iltutmish and Qabacha over the latter's possession of Lahore, Tabarhind and Kuharm until in 614 AH (1217 A.D.) the latter was finally defeated and ousted from the Punjab.[36]

In the meanwhile, Chengiz Khan had laid waste the great cities of the Middle East. Jalaluddin Mankbarni, the eldest son of the Khwarazm Shah, trying to escape the tightening noose, reached the Indus valley. The Punjab became a seething cauldron owing to the struggles of the armies of Qabacha, Mankbarni and the great Khan. Iltutmish decided to wait and see which way the tide of fortune turned. Nothing is known about the way he received the emissaries of Chengiz Khan or what he said to them, but as long as Chengiz was alive--he died in 1227--Iltutmish was careful not to alienate him. Eventually, Mankbarni left India and in 1228 Qabacha, hard pressed by Iltutmish, preferred to drown himself rather than surrender. It was the good fortune of India that Chengiz Khan noticing the portents revealed by burning a sheep's shoulder blades decided to retire the way he had come rather than through north India as he had originally planned.[37]

Conquests

Iltutmish's life was a study in continuous motion. He was always either fighting Hindu or Muslim chiefs in an effort to consolidate the empire and make the throne secure. From Lakhnauti in Bengal, where he secured the subjection of the Khilji ruler, Ghiyasuddin Iwaz, to the impregnable fort of Ranthambore in Rajasthan, which according to Minhaj, "for its exceeding strength, solidity and impregnability is famous and notorious throughout Hindustan. They have narrated in the Chronicles of the people of Hind after this manner, that seventy kings and more had appeared (at various times) at the foot of its walls, and not one of them had been able to reduce it." Thus, Iltutmish roamed restlessly attacking, subjugating, until practically the whole of northern India lay at his feet.[38]

As if to put a seal of approval on all these achievements and confirm the Sultan as owner of the conquered territories, the Caliph honoured him by sending emissaries carrying "honours, rich and ample. . . . On Monday, the 22nd of the month of Rabi-ul-Awwal, 626 AH [1129 A.D.] they reached the capital. The city was decorated [for the occasion] and the maliks, his sons--may they rest in peace--and other maliks, his suite and slaves likewise were honoured through this policy (on the part) of the Khalifah's court."[39]

The decorations must have been in the usual Eastern tradition--decking shops by hanging out rich shawls, brocades, fine dresses and all kinds of costly merchandise and even their women's jewellery, lamps and flags, attached to cords, drawn out across the streets, and the middle and lower portions of private buildings painted in gay colours. The Tabakat-i-Akbari, Ferishta and others say that arches and domes--*Kubbahs*--were also erected on this joyful occasion. Iltutmish, in his turn, bestowed robes of honour on the Caliph's emissaries and his own chiefs and nobles.[40]

Misfortunes were not far away, however, and in the same year the Sultan's eldest son and heir, Nasiruddin Mahmud Shah, died and Balka Malik-i-Husam-ud-Din Iwaz Khalji raised the flag of rebellion Lakhnauti. Iltutmish was thus back on the trail subjugating the rebel khalji and placing Ala-ud-Din Jani in his place.[41]

After a siege of eleven months he captured the fort of Gwalior in 630 AH (1223 A.D.). In 1235 A.D. he captured the fortress of Malwah and the town of Bhilsa demolishing the temple which had taken 300 years to build. From there he procceded to Ujjain and pillaged the temple, carrying back the statue of king Bikramajit (from whom the Vikram era dates), and other idols of metal and stone to Delhi.

Death

On the campaign to Banyan, he fell ill and returned to Delhi, entering the city seated in a covered litter at a time chosen by astrologers. However, the illness took its toll and on Monday, the 20th of Shaba'n, in the year 633 AH (April 29, 1236) he died, having ruled for a period of 26 years.[42]

Achievements

Iltutmish was a brave warrior and a shrewd, cautious and far-seeing statesman. It was his energy and application to carefully chosen objectives that converted fragmented pieces of conquered land into the compact and well-knit Sultanate of Delhi. He used *iqtas* as an instrument of liquidating the earlier Hindu setup, and linking the far- flung reaches of the empire to each other. Although in his reign *iqtas* were given mostly to Turks he made it a bureaucratic office so that dismissals and transfers became an accepted part of the system. He realised the economic potential of the fertile Doaba plain and, by settling a large number of Turks there, he gave Delhi its commercial and administrative control.

As king he was on his own with no traditions to guide him and unlike Qutbuddin Aibak, he had no Muizuddin Ghuri to back him. The result was that he cut Delhi off from Ghur and Ghazni and established a totally Indian independent empire with no vital links to any foreign kingdom.[43]

Iltutmish was intensely religious and spent a part of the night in prayer and meditation before sleeping. He always protected and paid respects to the various Sufi saints, such as Shaikh Qutbuddin Bakhtiyar

Kaki and Shaikh Bahauddin Zakariya, though he also used this connection with the saints to further his political objectives. For instance, Zakariya's support helped him in the conquest of Multan, and the agricultural extension scheme of giving land to Sufis made the saints a buffer between the local people and the new rulers. He also saw the advantage of keeping the Hindus appeased and was never harsh with them.

His handling of Chengiz Khan and Mankbarni were proof of his diplomatic skills which resulted in the strengthening of the throne of Delhi.[44] His genius created the city of Delhi in a way that was to last until 1857--a city of beautiful buildings that was to become a centre of learning and culture. The city was so magnificent that in the literature of the time it was called Hazrat-i-Delhi or just Shehr, a city.

The Mongol conquest had disrupted, among other things, the slave traffic. Some slaves, however, were brought to Iltutmish by the sea route. These, having been brought from a region between Anatolia and Turkestan, were considered Turkish, and deemed themselves equal and brothers of the other Turks, and after Iltutmish's death, called themselves as Sultani, the slaves or, rather, the officers of the Sultan whom they had put upon the throne. There is no mention in contemporary accounts of the appointment of any India-born Muslim by Iltutmish, so the throne was a purely Turkish throne supported by Turkish nobles. However, Hindu chiefs were made feudatories and confirmed in their administration by the Sultan. The fiefs were obviously hereditary and their chiefs were bound to pay tribute and maintain law and order.[45]

Iltutmish had been chosen king because of his even temper and outstanding achievements. Even so, he was so awed by his peers, the Qutbi and Muizzi maliks that he used to say that when he saw them standing in his court he felt inclined to come down from the throne and kiss their hands and feet.[46]

However, he refused to be overpowered by them and was very much his own man. After the death of his eldest son and heir-apparent, Nasiruddin Mahmud Shah to whom he had shown special honour such as sending him a costly dress and a red umbrella after receiving the robes of honour from the Caliph in 1229, he appointed his daughter Raziya his successor. So ably had she discharged her duties as regent during his absence in the Gwalior campaign and so much faith did he have in her and her mother, Turkan Khatun, that on his return, he ordered his *mushrif-i-mamlakat* to prepare a decree naming her his heir. While the decree was being prepared the amirs protested but Iltutmish went ahead saying "my sons are engrossed in the pleasures of youth and none of them possesses the capability of managing the affairs of the country. After my death it will be seen that no one of them will be found more worthy of the heir-apparentship than she, my daughter."

When he was struck down by his last illness, however, he brought his second son, Rukn-ud-Din Firuz, along with him. This young man had received the fief of Badaun and later of Lahore. He was also given a green Canopy of State. His mother, Shah Turkan, according to Minhaj, was a Turkish "hand-maid and the head (woman) of all the Sultan's harem and great was the bounty, benevolence and charity of that Malikah towards ulemas, Saiyyids, priests and recluses." Whether it was this generosity which brought important people to her side or whether Iltutmish changed his mind at the last moment is not clear but after the latter's death "the maliks and grandees of the kingdom, by agreement, seated Rukn-ud-Din upon the throne on Tuesday, the 21st of the month Shabaan 633 H [April 30, 1236] and the diadem and throne acquired beauty and splendour from his dignity and excellence and elegance; and all rejoiced at his accession, and donned honorary dresses [to testify their joy]."[47]

RUKN-UD-DIN FIRUZ SHAH

However, as soon as he was crowned and the powerful nobles, who had helped place him on the throne, had returned to their posts the Sultan gave free rein to his profligate inclinations. He "opened the door of his treasuries, and gave himself up to pleasure, and began to expend in the most profuse fashion, the funds of the *Bait-ul-Mal* in an improper manner. Such was his excessive appetite for pleasure and several enjoyments, that the business of the country, the concerns of the State and the regulation of the affairs of the country fell into a state of disorder and confusion."[48]

He loved riding elephants and, in a state of intoxication, would ride through the bazaars of the city scattering *tankhas* of red gold which the people clamoured to pick up. His liberality knew no bounds and he conferred more honorary dresses and presents than any other king. However, as Minhaj writes ". . . . his misfortune was this, that his inclinations were wholly towards buffoonery, sensuality and diversion and that he was entirely enslaved by dissipation and debauchery, and most of his honorary dresses were made to such people as musicians and singers, buffoons and Ganymedes."[49]

While the son thus indulged himself, the mother also showed her real colours. Perhaps, as Minhaj surmises, she had been jealous of the other ladies of the harem during her husband's lifetime but could do nothing to hurt them. Now as queen mother she decided to avenge herself. She became tyrannical and autocratic towards those who may have hurt her in any way and even managed to destroy some of them. Both mother and son caused a younger son of Iltutmish Kutb-ud-Din who, according to Minhaj, was a youth of great worth and promise (and so to be feared as a potential rival), to be blinded and put to death.[50]

These activities upset the nobles in different parts of the empire and they started manifesting their hostility to the sovereign in various ways. Ghiyas-ud-Din Muhammad Shah, a younger brother of Rukn-ud-Din Firuz Shah, who held the iqta of Awadh, took possession of the whole treasure of Lakhnauti, which was on its way to Delhi, and then plundered several towns. Malik Izz-ud-Din Muhammad Salari, the feudatory of Badaun, rebelled while the maliks Izz-ud-Din Kabir Khan-ai-Ayaz, Saif-ud-Din Kuji and Ala-ud-Din Jani, the feudatories of Multan, Hansi and Lahore respectively, also joined together in rebellion against the ruler.[51]

Rukn-ud-Din moved his army out of the capital as a show of force to cow down his enemies but was deserted by his wazir, Nizam-ul-mulk Muhammad Junaidi, who joined Izz-ud-Din Muhammad Salari, both of them then joining Malik Jani and Malik Kuji.

The army moved towards Kuhran, and the Turkish Amirs and slaves of the household who were serving with the contingents forming the centre followed, and in the vicinity of Mansurpur and Tarain, they killed a number of high officials and the sons of others. These included Taj-ul-mulk Mahmud, the Dabir (Secretary), the son of the *Mushrif-i-Mamalik*, Baha-ud-Din Hasan-i-Ashari; Karim-ud-Din-i-Zahid, Ziya-ul-mulk, the son of Nizam-ul-mulk Muhammad Junaidi and a number of other Tajzik officials.[52] This seems to have been a case of settling scores by the Ilbari Turks with their non-Turkish rivals.

In the meanwhile, in the month of Rabi-ul-Awwal in the year 634 H, Raziya entered into open hostility with the Queen mother who had stayed in the capital, forcing Rukn-ud-Din Firuz Shah to turn back. Taking full advantage of the chaotic conditions, Raziya accused Shah Trukan of conspiring to put her to death. Clad in a red garment, customary for the aggrieved, she appeared before the people gathered at the mosque for Friday prayers and, in the name of her father, appealed for help against the machinations of her step mother. In the Futuh-us-Salatin,

Isami recounts that she appealed to the people saying she should be given a chance to prove her abilities and if she did not prove herself better than the men her head should be struck off.[53]

The people moved by her plea, attacked the royal palace and seized Shah Turkan. When Rukn-ud-Din reached the city he found it in revolt with his mother already in prison. The centre contingents of the Delhi forces and the Turkish Amirs then entered Delhi to join Raziya, pledging their allegiance and placing her on the throne with the title of Sultan.[54]

Raziya immediately despatched a force consisting of Turkish slaves and Amirs to *Kilu-Ghari* where the Sultan had his palace. He was captured and brought to the city where he was imprisoned and "received the Almighty's mercy". His seizure, imprisonment and death took place on Sunday, the 18th of the month of Rabi-ul-Awwal, in the year 634 H (November 9, 1236 AD), his reign having lasted for 6 months and 26 days.[55]

Notes

1. R.C. Majumdar, H.C. Raychaudhuri & K. Datta, *An Advanced History of India,* p. 279. Hereinafter referred to as Majumdar.
2. Minhaj-us-Siraj, *Tabaqat-i-Nasiri,* p. 370. Hereinafter referred to as Minhaj.
3. Majumdar, p. 277.
4. Minhaj, p. 377.
5. Ibid., p. 451.
6. Ibid., pp. 460.
7. Ibid., pp. 465-469.
8. Majumdar, p. 277.
9. A.B.M. Habibullah, *The Foundation of Muslim Rule in India*, pp. 54-56.
10. Majumdar, p. 279.
11. M. Habib, *Politics and Society during the early Medieval Period*, p. 105.
12. Minhaj, p. 506.
13. Majumdar, p. 281.
14. Minhaj, p. 512.
15. Ibid., pp. 525-526.
16. Ibid., p. 513.
17. Ibid., p. 513.
18. Ibid., pp. 514-520.
19. Ibid., p. 528.
20. Minhaj-us-Siraj, *Tabaqat-i-Nasiri,* edited and translated by Major H.G. Raverty, p. 528, footnote 3. Hereinafter referred to as Raverty.
21. Ibid., p. 529, footnote 4.
22. Ibid., pp. 529-530.
23. Ibid., p. 529, footnote 4.
24. Ibid., pp. 529-530. footnote 4.
25. Ibid., p. 517, footnote 4.
26. M. Habib & K.A. Nizami ed., *A Comprehensive History of India*, p. 20. Hereinafter referred to as Habib & Nizami.

27. Ibid., p. 209, footnote 4.
28. Minhaj, pp. 599-600.
29. Ibid., pp. 598-599.
30. Ibid., pp. 600-604.
31. Habib & Nizami, p. 213.
32. Ibid., p. 47.
33. Minhaj, p. 607.
34. Ibid., p. 607, footnote 5.
35. Habib & Nizami, p. 214.
36. Minhaj, p. 607.
37. Habib & Nizami, pp. 215-218.
38. Minhaj, pp. 610-615.
39. Ibid., pp. 616.
40. Ibid., p. 616, footnotes 3 & 4.
41. Ibid., pp. 617-618.
42. Ibid., pp. 620-623.
43. Habib & Nizami, pp. 226-227.
44. Ibid., pp. 229-230.
45. Ibid., pp. 224-225.
46. Barani, *Tarikh-i-Firuz Shahi* (Elliot and Dowson, Vol. III)
47. Minhaj, pp. 631-632.
48. Ibid., p. 632.
49. Ibid., p. 636.
50. Ibid., p. 633.
51. Ibid., pp. 633-634.
52. Ibid., pp. 633-635.
53. Ibn Batuta: *The Rehla of Ibn-Batuta*, Tr by A. Mohd Husain, Baroda, 1953.
54. Minhaj, p. 636.
55. Ibid., p. 636.

2

SULTAN RAZIYA

SULTAN RAZIYA

Raziya had now achieved what her father desired for her. She was a crowned sovereign with the title of Sultan, with the royal suffix ud-Duniya wa-ud-Din and in a position to make full use of the statecraft she had learnt under the tutelage of her father when she had lived with him in the Kushk-i-Firuzi (royal palace), where her mother, Turkan Khatun had been the greatest of the ladies of the harem. Even though she had lived in purdah, her abilities had been amply evident during her father's absence in Gwalior.[1]

The state religion was the Sunni creed of Islam. The other Islamic sects like the Kiramitah and the Mulahidah were considered heretical and were abhorrent to the Sunnis. However, they were deeply entrenched in the country and flourishing in places like Sind, Multan and Gujarat and even round Delhi and the Doaba area. Soon after Raziya's accession Nur-ud-Din, a Turk, who was styled Nur the Turk, incited these sects to revolt against the new sovereign. A secret pact of loyalty was concluded between members of these sects and Nur Turk who openly denounced the Ulema as Murji (procrastinators) and Nasibi (setters-up) and whipped up the populace into a frenzy of rage against the ecclesiastical establishment. On Friday, the 6th of Rajab, 634 H (March 1237) about 1000 armed heretics entered the Jama Masjid. They came in two groups, one entering the mosque from the northern side and the second passing through the Bazar-i-Bazazan (cloth merchants bazar) entered into the Muizzi College mistaking it for the mosque. In the melee a number of people were killed by the sword-bearing intruders while many others were trampled underfoot. However, the rebellion was soon suppressed since, on hearing of the event, the warriors of the city such as Nasir-ud-Din, Ai-Yitim and Amir Imam-i-Nasiri, the poet, rode fully armed into the mosque through the Minarah entrance and slaughtered the rebels. Worshippers who had fled to the roof top joined in the fray by throwing bricks and stones on the heads of the rebels who were thus effectively crushed.[2]

Furthermore, though Raziya had managed to restore normalcy after the chaos created by her brother Rukn-ud-Din, a number of Amirs ranged themselves against her. Chief among these was the Nizam-ul-mulk Muhammad Junaidi who, with other Amirs, such as Malik Ala-ud-Din Jani, Malik Saif-ud-Din Kuji, Malik Izz-ud-Din, Kabir Khan-i-Ayaz, Malik Izz-ud-Din, and Muhammad Salari gathered at the gates of Delhi and started hostilities against her. At her command, Malik Nusrat-ud-Din Ta-yasai, the feudatory of Awadh, marched to her aid, but after he had crossed the Ganga, the hostile Maliks who were beseiging Delhi marched towards his camp and took him captive.[3] He appears to have been suffering from an illness when he had received the Sultan's command and so succumbed to the disease and died.[4]

This siege of Delhi continued for some time and then Raziya came out of her city and established camp on the banks of the Jamuna where several pitched battles took place between those loyal to her and her enemies. Maliks Izz-ud-Din Muhammad Salari and Izz-ud-Din Kabir Khan-Ayaz switched allegiance to her, and in a joint secret conclave decided that the Maliks Jani, Saif-ud-Din Kuji and the Nizam-ul-Mulk Muhammad Junaidi be summoned to her presence and captured and imprisoned, so that the rebellion could be crushed. Getting a hint of this the Maliks fled, but were chased by the royal horsemen and eliminated by being killed in battle, or perhaps, by strangulation in prison. Ala-ud-Din Jani's head was brought to the capital, but the Nizam-ul-Mulk managed to escape to the hills of Sirmur Bardar where he died a natural death.[5]

With the rebellion thus subdued, peace returned to the kingdom and Raziya began the task of appointing important office bearers. Khwaja Muhazzab, the former deputy to the Nizam-ul-Mulk, now became Wazir and received the title of Nizam-ul-Mulk. The charge of the army, of which she was head, went to Malik Saif-ud-Din, I-bak-i-Bihaq, who received the title of Kutlugh Khan, while Malik Izz-ud-Din Kabir Khan-i-Ayaz received the fief of Lahore. All the Amirs in the empire extended their loyalty to the Sultan and paid homage.[6]

All seemed well when suddenly the Commander of the Army, Malik

Saif-ud-Din, I-bak-i-Bihaq, died and the charge was given to Malik Qutb-ud-Din Hasan (in certain places he is called Husain). Almost immediately after his appointment, he was sent to relieve the fort of Ranthambore to which the Rajputs had laid siege soon after the death of Iltutmish. He freed the fortress, destroyed the works and marched back to the capital, making no effort to secure the stronghold.[7]

In the meantime the Sultan had appointed Malik-i-Kabir Ikhtiyar-ud-Din Aet-kin to the important post of *Amir-i-Hajib* and showed favour to Malik Jamal-ud-Din Ya-kut who was known as the Habashi (Ethiopian) because of his country of origin, and who held the post of Amir-i-Akhur, Lord of the stables. What the favour was, Minhaj does not specify except to say that it was to be "in attendance upon the Sultan". It certainly was not a promotion, for Yakut had been an incumbent of the post even before Raziya's accession to the throne. But, according to Minhaj, this aroused the envy of the Turkish nobles. At the same time, Raziya decided to don a male costume and to come out of purdah riding unveiled through the streets so that everyone could see her.[8]

This, perhaps, increased the sense of insecurity of the Turkish king makers, since firstly, she dared to show favour to a non-Turk and then she appeared in a manly garb, no doubt with the idea of impressing on them the fact that she was no retiring female but a woman who could deal with men on their own terms. The change of garb actually consisted only of assuming the tunic and head-dress of a man, which was the only difference between the dress of men and women at that time, the rest of the garments being exacity the same, but even that was enough to underscore her defiance of traditions specifying the role of women.

Next, Raziya sent her troops to Gwalior. The city had already had a governor appointed by Iltutmish and Minhaj was the Kazi. When the fortress had been relieved by her forces earlier, the governor had died and a new feudatory, Amir-i-Dad Ziya-ud-Din Junaidi had been appointed. But being a kinsman of the rebel Wazir he may have been suspected of disloyalty and was recalled to Delhi along with some other persons, including Minhaj, who probably did not relish leaving the city because he uses the phrase, "As disobedience was out of the question, this servant of the victorious kingdom came out of the fortress. . . . and returned to Dihli the capital." This has led writers to assume that he was under some sort of a cloud, but when he reached Delhi, he was appointed head of the Nasiriah College at the capital while retaining the Kaziship of Gwalior.[9]

But, Raziya like her father, was never to be left in peace. In 637 H

(1239 AD) Malik Izz-ud-Din, Kabir Khan-i-Ayaz, the feudatory of Lahore, rebelled. The Sultan herself, at the head of her army, advanced into the Punjab against the rebellious Malik who retreated before her advance, going towards the Indus until he reached Sudharah and could go no further for fear of falling into hostile hands. He made his submission after the royal army had crossed the Ravi but was deprived of the fief of Lahore receiving the charge of Multan instead, the feudatory of the latter city, Malik Ikhtiyar-ud-Din Karakush Khan being sent to Lahore. After this arrangement, Raziya returned to Delhi.[10]

The next rebellion was that of the feudatory of Tabarhindah, Malik Ikhtiyar-ud-Din Altuniah, who had received his first fief of Baran from Raziya herself on her accession to the throne. He was secretly abetted in his rebellion by some court nobles. Again, Raziya set out to confront the new rebel. But when she reached Tabarhindah, the Turkish nobles rose against her, killed Yakut and imprisoned her in the fortress of Tabarhindah.[11]

When news of her imprisonment reached Delhi her brother, Muiz-ud-Din Bahram Shah, was placed on the throne. When the Maliks and Amirs, who had betrayed Raziya returned to Delhi, they paid public homage to the new ruler and pledged their allegiance on the condition of the Deputyship being conferred on Malik Ikhityar-ud-Din Aet Kin. Very soon the new deputy, together with the Wazir, the Nizamul-mulk, the Khwaja Muhazzab-ud-Din Muhammad-i-Iwaz, the Mustaufi, took over the control of state affairs.

Soon this intrusion into his sovereignty began to irk the new Sultan, especially when, after his marriage to a divorced sister of the Sultan, the deputy assumed the prerogatives of royalty like the triple naubat (Kettledrums and other instruments sounded at stated periods of the day before the gates of sovereigns and great men for which he had requested permission) and the stationing of an elephant at the entrance of his residence to which he had no right. He indulged in opulent living and became autocratic until Muiz-ud-Din sought means of getting rid of him. Towards this end, he ordered a discourse to be delivered at the palace and, on its termination, he sent two Turks who were trained as Fidais or assassins and who, in front of the dais in the audience hall, stabbed Aet-kin to death and badly wounded the Wazir although he survived. Since it was Aet-kin who had incited Altuniah to revolt against Raziya, in a way he could be said to have deserved his fate.[12]

In the meanwhile, in a surprise move, Raziya, while in jail in Tabarhindah, had married Altuniah. Now allied matrimonially and politically, the two moved out of the fortress at the head of an army and headed towards Delhi to recapture her throne. Maliks Izz-ud-Din Muhammad Salari and Karakush rebelled against Bahram Shah and left Delhi to join Raziya and Altuniah. Bahram Shah moved out of the capital at the head of his army to meet the advancing troops. As has happened so often during the course of Indian history, the troops of the rebels deserted and joined the Sultan's army. When they reached Kaithal, the newly married couple fell into the hands of the Hindus and were killed. The date of the defeat was the 24th of the month of Rabi-ul-Awwal in 638 H (13th October 1240). Both were killed the next day. Raziya had been queen for a periods of 3 years, 6 months and 6 days.[13]

Ibn Batuta gives the following description of Raziya's death, ".... Raziya was defeated and obliged to fly. Pressed by hunger and overcome by fatigue, she addressed herself to a man engaged in cultivating the ground and begged for food. He gave her a bit of bread which she devoured and then was overpowered by sleep. She was dressed in the garment of a man but when the peasant looked at her as she slept he perceived under her upper garment a tunic trimmed with gold and pearls. Seeing (that) she was a woman he killed her, stripped her of valuables, drove away her horse and buried her corpse in his field. He then carried some of her garments to the market for sale. The dealers suspected him and took him before the Magistrate, who caused him to be beaten. The wretch then confessed that he had killed Raziya and told his guards where he had buried her. They exhumed her body, washed it and wrapping it in a shroud buried it again in the same place. A small shrine was erected over her grave which is visited by pilgrims and is considered a place of sanctity. It is situated on the banks of the Jamuna."[14] How far Ibn Batuta is correct in his account is problematic, since his account of Raziya's life, --"She was eventually suspected of intimacy with one of her slaves, an Abyssinian by birth, and the people resolved upon deposing her and giving her a husband. So, she was deposed and married to one of her relations, and her brother Nasir-ud-Din obtained the supreme power. But Raziya and her husband revolted against him." -- is hardly noted for its accuracy.[15]

A dilapidated black marble tomb standing some distance inside Turkman Gate of the city of Shahjehanabad (now called old Delhi) was considered to be her burial place, until the Archaeological Department very recently declared it to be that of a Sufi saint.

Notes

1. Minhaj-us-Siraj, *Tabaqat-i-Nasiri*, p. 638. Hereinafter referred to as Minhaj.
2. Ibid., pp. 646-647.
3. Ibid., pp. 639-640.
4. Minhaj-us-Siraj: *Tabaqat-i-Nasiri*, edited and translated by Major H.G. Raverty, p. 640, footnote 1. Hereinafter referred to as Raverty.
5. Minhaj, pp. 640-641.
6. Ibid., p. 641.
7. Ibid., pp. 642-643, Raverty, p. 642, footnote 1.
8. Ibid., pp. 642-643.
9. Ibid., p. 643, Raverty, p. 643, footnote 4.
10. Ibid., pp. 644-645, Raverty, p. 644, footnote 7.
11. Ibid., p. 647.
12. Ibid, pp. 649-651, Raverty, footnotes 4 & 7.
13. Ibid., p. 648.
14. Elliot & Dowson, *History of India as Told by its Own Historians*, Vol. III, p. 593.
15. Ibid., pp. 592-593.

3

THE SULTAN'S HOUSEHOLD

During the early years the main problems facing the ruling dynasty were those of expansion and defence i.e. purely military. Planning and setting up of institutions could only follow consolidation and firm establishment of the ruling class.The institutions and practices brought by the Turks through Persia and Ghazni, prevailed in the newly conquered territories at the higher levels of administration. At the level of revenue collection and local goverment, local practices continued to flourish not being noticeably interfered or altered with. These institutions were, of course, already known to Indians since they had already been functioning in the Punjab under the Ghaznavid viceroys.[1]

The only firm and fixed basis of the State was its Islamic character although, the supposed rulers of the Muslim world (no matter how far its boundaries extended), the Caliphs of Baghdad, had lost all power. Still, in fiction, they remained its nominal head and no emperor, however powerful, could rule in any but the Caliph's name. His name was always mentioned in the *Khutba* (sermon delivered after congregational prayers) and inscribed on the *sikka* (coins) which, along with the taraz (the sovereign's name embroidered or woven on cloth) and the umbrella, formed the symbol of Muslim royalty. Thus all rulers, including those who had received no formal delegation of power from him, were regarded as being viceroys of the Caliph. A formal recognition, as in the case of Iltutmish, added extra dignity and was the mark of legalisation of a kingdom. Even after the last Abbasid Caliph lost his life at the hands of the Mughals his name continued on coins and *khutba* of far-flung kingdoms. In India, the name was inscribed in the local script to make sure that the conquered people would know that they were part of a world wide empire.[2]

THE SULTAN

In reality, of course, the king was supreme, his power curbed only by demands of expediency and the Shariah (muslim law). The latter could always be interpreted in a way to make even the most despotic and arbitrary king seem to be following the Holy writ. To this end, ecclesiastics, and *mullahs*, were kept happy and placated so that they could put the best interpretation on the worst actions of the monarch.The temporal authority thus rested in the sovereign,while the spiritual resided in the Shaikh-ul-Islam, the highest ecclesiast in the land.[3]

The administrative set-up was, of necessity, a powerful machine forming a triangle with the monarch at the apex and the lowest functionaries forming the base.

A powerful and conscientious ruler was an extremely busy and hardworking man, constantly engaged in warfare, discussions and consultations, overseeing the work of officers and departments. If he wished to keep the reins of government firmly in his own hands he had to be highly visible, making himself available to listen to complaints and redress grievances while maintaining the aloofness and distance required to inspire awe and reverence in his subjects. Pomp was a necessary adjunct of power and was used to impress subjects, allies and foes alike. The holding of *durbars* was a political necessity. In surroundings of opulence and splendour the monarch himself, with his clothes and jewels, shone like the sun overawing even ambassadors to the extent that according to Barani, some were known to faint in the royal presence.[4]

Early Islam, of course, had no concept of monarchy. The four Caliphs following the Prophet were elected by consensus and ruled by it. Khilafat literally means succession, and a person who succeeds is called the Khalifa (written by westerners as Caliph). The Khalifa was looked upon as a person holding religious office, but he was not like the Pope who is regarded as being a successor to St. Peter.

The *Majlis-i-Am,* the durbar, a Persian institution, became a Delhi tradition. It was a public court of the highest administrative organ where the Sultan transacted all affairs of the State, sitting upon the throne with the *chattri* (the royal umbrella) and *Durbash* (royal baton) conspicuously displayed. Elephants and the naubat (beating of drums) were the exclusive privilege of the Sultan as were the black and red joint canopies.[5]

The Khalifa in Islam had no power to frame rules of religion.[6] It was Caliph Muawiyah (661-680 AD) who turned the Caliphate into a monarchy by naming his son Yazid his successor, while retaining the title of

Caliph. Later Caliphs and Sultans continued the practice. Muawiyah also instituted the leading Arab tribes as an exclusive governing class. The Omayyad (661-750 AD) could control the whole Muslim empire but their successors, the Abbasids, could not control the Arab countries who, one after the other, declared their independence. By the year 900 AD the Caliphate was left with its eastern lands-Persians and Turks--designated conveniently as Ajam.

Mahmud of Ghazni (998-1030 AD), after his spectacular conquests both of India and Ajam, came to be known as the first Sultan of Ajam. It was after his rise that the Caliphate became a purely formal symbol until its extinction by the Mughals.[7]

THE COURT

The Turks had been Persianised in thought and behaviour long before coming to India. It was from Persia that they derived the theories of Kingship, zil-e-subhani (shadow of God), court etiquette and administrative and military set ups. Pre-muslim Persian heroes such as Kaikhusru, Jamshed etc. became a part of the muslim ethos and were lauded by muslim poets and writers.

The court of Delhi was a copy of the Sassanid court and the customs of pabos and zaminbos--kissing the feet of the ruler and the ground in front of him--were introduced. The Persian New Year--Navroz--was celebrated with pomp and gaiety. The king, being given the title of *niyabat-i-khudawandi*-viceroy of God-achieved a touch of divinity. The ulema produced hadises, traditions of the Prophet such as "Obey God, Obey the Prophet and Obey those with authority" and exhortations to obey the ruler "even if he be a negro or a slave or mutilated in form" to further this image of the monarch and to transform him into something superhuman.

In the Siyasat-namah, Nizam-ul-mulk stresses on the kings, since they are divinely appointed, the need for keeping the subjects in such a position "that they know their stations and never remove the ring of servitude from their ears." It sees the relationship between the ruler and ruled as one of tension; any latitude given to subjects is seen to diminish the majesty of the ruler and lead to rebelliousness. The Ghaznavid Sultans therefore denied their subjects even a limited right of self-defence, because they feared that arms turned against invaders could well be turned against the Sultan himself. They viewed the division as being all the rulers on one side and the ruled on the other. It was because of this that Mahmud reprimanded the people of Balkh when, in 396 AH (1006 AD) they resisted the Qarakhanid general, Jafartigin. In the determined resistance, royal property was damaged and this invoked Mahmud's wrath. He told the townspeople that they had no right to resist the enemy and so place his own property in jeopardy; subjects must resign themselves to whichever ruler proved himself to be strongest. It was for the army to fight, and subjects should not arrogate this funtion to themselves. They should not allow feelings of loyalty to stand in the way of protecting themselves from getting the best possible terms from the incoming power. It was in view of this that Masud, Mahmud's son, left for India in the face of a threatened Seljuq attack leaving his officials behind in Ghazna to make terms with the incomers with whom they might expect to find employment.[8]

Slaves were recruited and trained according to Persian traditions and the armies had the same discipline and arms as the Sassanid warriors.

Names of individuals and institutions were Persian and though the Turks may have spoken to each other in their language. Turki, the official language was Persian and all important work was done in that language.[9]

THE ROYAL HOUSEHOLD

All this pomp and grandeur, naturally entailed the employment of a large staff. The royal household was of pre-eminent importance not only because it was the Sultan's base and therefore played an important part in the administrative machinery of the State, but because there was no clear-cut distinction between the Sultan's wealth and public funds.

The controller of the huge establishment, the *Wakil-i-dar*, was a man of rank and prestige. He supervised payments of allowances and salaries and oversaw everything-the royal kitchen, the sharabkhana (wine cellars) the stables and even the harem. All royal commands relating to the household were relayed through him and the household and those dependent on it had to approach him for all their needs. All affairs requiring royal sanction were reported by him to the king. Apart from being a good administrator he also had to be a man of great circumspection and tact. [10] Since most of the persons he had dealings with had direct access to the Sultan all his reports had to be precisely worded and carefully weighed.

Almost equal in rank was the Amir hajib, also called Barbek, who was master of ceremonies at court. It was he who marshalled all nobles and officials according to their rank and ensured the dignity of royal functions. No one could enter the presence of the Sultan without being introduced by his assistants, the hajibs, who also conveyed messages from the Sultan to supplicants and officials. All petitions were also presented through the amir and his subordinates. The Naib Barbek, the Amir's deputy, was in charge of making arrangements for the more important celebrations. Occasionally the naib, along with some other officials would be left to act as the Sultan's deputy during the latter's absence from the capital. Both Amir and Naib had, naturally, to be selected from among princes of royal blood or officers close to the king.

Most of the hajibs were trained soldiers and could be appointed to command expeditions. On the field, they acted as ADCs to the Sultan. some would be invited to attend the council of war and their counsel would be listened to; others would be entrusted with the task of making inventories of the presents received by the Sultan. As such, they were important officials of State, not merely courtiers or household officers.[11]

The ushers, or Naqibs, were used to proclaim orders to soldiers and the people. They ran in front of the royal processions announcing in a loud voice the approach of the Sultan. Their chief, the *Naqib-ul-muqaba,* whose insignia of office consisted of a gold mace, and a gold tiara surrounded with peacock feathers, sat on a platform leading into the hall of audience and scrutinised every newcomer. He and his assistants delivered the formal eulogies on occasions of feasts and celebrations.[12]

The bodyguards, known as *Jandars*, consisted of tall, handsome brave young men who were picked with great care both for their appearance and their valour. Because they had to be present on all occasions when the Sultan appeared in public, special attention was paid to their uniforms. They were picked from slaves of proven loyalty and were commanded by a trustworthy noble styled the Sar-jandar. A second body of fully armed soldiers, the *Silahdars,* led by the *Sar-silahdar* also attended the Sultan. The umbrella bearers were led by their chief, the Sar-chatradar.

The female quarters were guarded by eunuchs who acted as messengers between the harem and the outer world and attended the Sultan when he visited the harem. They were privileged people and, occasionally, those with special qualities of valour or statesmanship would be raised to high positions such as general, as in the case of Malik Ambar and Malik Kafur.[13]

The rest of the palace staff consisted of the librarian (Kitabdar); the kitchen supervisor and food taster (Chasnigir); the *Sharabdar*, who was in charge of the cellars from where the liquor was served by the *saqi-i-khas*. The *Mashaldar* was in charge of the lights and the *Farash* of furniture and tents. The royal writing case was kept by the *dawatdar* while the *Khazindar* was the keeper of the privy purse.[14]

The Gurbeg was in charge of the armour, except the Sultan's special armour and personal arms which were in the charge of the *Khasab-dar*, while the Amir-i-tuzuk looked after the royal insignia. The Sultan was helped in his ablutions by the *Tashdar* (ewer-bearer), while the Agachi attended to his personal needs. There was of course an eminent physician, the *Malik-i-hukama*, to attend to royal medical needs. The registrar of the palace was titled *Dabir-i-sara*.[15]

Any institution, the size of the royal household would, of necessity, require a large and efficient commissariat. This was divided into departments called Karkhanas (workshops) and manufacturing units were set up not only for making clothes, shoes and other articles of everyday use but also for producing items like manuscripts and paintings. Karkhanas, known as *Ratibis*, dealt with perishable goods such as food for the kitchen and kennels, fodder for the stables and oil for lamps.

The *Ghair-ratibi karkhanas* supplied clothes, uniforms, furniture, tents etc. Each was supervised by a Malik or Khan and had a *Mutassarif* who was responsible for the accounts and acted as the immediate supervisor. Requisitions from all karkhanas were sent to the chief Mutassarif concerned.

Of the ratibi karkhanas, the Paigahs or horse breeding department, was the most extensive since the army had to be well supplied with horses. Arab, Turkish and Russian horses were the most valued as presents to be given and received. The Akhurbeg, or the superintendent of royal horses, was one of the most important officials of the State.[16]

Elephants were also greatly valued and played such a decisive role in battle that the Sultan never allowed any noble or feudatory to have too many of them. They were housed in royal stables under an important functionary called the Shahnah-i-fil. Bullocks, camels mules and buffaloes were kept for transport purposes.[17]

Hunting, provided recreation and also kept the army in a state of readiness. On occasions of grand hunts, the Sultans marched in battle array. Leopards, dogs, hawks and falcons were kept in various karkhanas for this sport. Large forests were reserved for the royal hunt near the capital itself, and other special areas in the provinces reserved for special game. The *Amir-i-shikar* directed this 'sport' department with various deputies and assistants.[18]

The Sultan's private parties were cultural levées, where the outstanding literati from the realm gathered. Poets, writers, historians and brilliant conversationalists all were invited.[19] In other parties music and dance were the main attractions. Wine would flow in both gatherings, in greater or lesser quantities, depending on the Sultan's inclinations.[20] These assemblies were known as the *Majlis-i-aish* (convivial assembly) and were meant solely for the entertainment of the Sultan. Amusements could include witnessing games such as elephant fighting; kite flying and wrestling matches.

The Majlis-i-khilwat, the Privy Council, was one to which the most trusted officials were invited and consulted on important matters of State.[21]

The Sultan's companions were paid salaries and given grants of land for the sole purpose of being companions or Nadims. Being so close to the sovereign was a great privilege and they, naturally, exerted great power. By their calibre could be measured the calibre of the king himself for, obviously, an intelligent hardworking king would surround himself with companions of a similar type while a weak, pleasure-loving monarch would choose people nearer his taste.[22]

Abul Fazal Baihaqi, 385-470 AH (995-1077 AD) had a long career as an official in the correspondence department of Sultan Masud, son of Mahmud of Ghazni. His Tarikh-i-Masudi gives a graphic day-to-day account of happenings in the *Ghaznavids* empire in a way that is rare among historians of the Middle East or the Indian subcontinent. He made copious notes and often made copies for his own use of diplomatic and official documents. He sifted and weighed conflicting evidence and presented events in a balanced and judicious manner. He was a personal witness to many of the events he recorded and his narrative has a freshness and immediacy lacking in others. Since no descriptions of the early Indian Sultans' durbars or day to day life are available it would be well to quote from Baihaqi to obtain a good idea of how the Sultans could spend their time.

Pomp & Grandeur

"The golden throne, the splendid carpet and the hall for audiences and merry-making which the Amir had ordered to be constructed and on which they had been busy for over 3 years was now ready. They informed the Amir and he ordered that they should instal and set it down (the throne) on the great dais of the new palace and put the building in order.

Everyone who on that day saw the adornment never saw anything after that which could compare with it. I was one of them at that time and I have never known anything like it. The throne was constructed entirely of red gold overlaid with shapes and patterns of branches and plant fronds. It was set with a large number of precious jewels. The throne itself was overlaid with covers of Rumi brocades. It had four well-filled cushions made of silk and sewn with gold thread, laid down for the feet; a cushion for the back and four other cushions, two for each side. A golden-plated chain hung from the ceiling of the chamber containing the dais, and came down over the dais where the crown and throne were. The crown was attached to this chain and there were four bronze figures, fashioned in the shape of human beings and mounted on columns which were secured to the throne itself, so that their hands were outstretched and thus held the crown safely. In this way the crown did not hurt, the chains and the columns supported it and the Sultan's cap could go underneath it. They draped this dais with rugs, gold-woven Rumi brocade and gold-woven parti-coloured carpets. Three hundred and eighty golden dishes were set out in the hall, each a *gaz* long and a *khushktar gaz* wide. Over these were placed cakes of camphor,vessels of musk, fragments of sandalwood and amber. Before the high throne were fixed fifteen settings of pomegranate-coloured and Badakhashani rubies, pearls and turquoises. Within the oppulently appointed hall they had set out a table and, in the middle of it, stretching towards the ceiling was a pavillion made of *halva* and there was ample other food."

"On Tuesday, the 21st of *Sha'ban*, the Amir, may God be pleased with him, came from the Mahmudi garden to this new palace and seated himself on his new golden throne on the dais. The crown was suspended above his cap and he wore a cloak of crimson brocade so heavily ornamented with gold that only a little of the material underneath could be seen. All round the hall, standing against the palace, were the household *ghulams* with robes of Saqlatun, Baghdadi and Isfahani cloth; two pointed caps; gold mounted waist sashes; pendents and gold maces in their hands. On the dais itself, to both right and left of the throne, were ten *ghulams*, with 4 sectioned caps on their heads, heavy bejewelled waist sashes and bejewelled sword belts. In the middle of the hall were two lines of *ghulams*; one line was standing against the wall wearing 4 sectioned caps. In their hands they held arrows and swords and they had quivers and bow-cases. There was another line, positioned down the centre of the hall, with two pointed caps, heavy silver mounted sashes, pendents and silver maces in their hands. The *ghulams* of both the lines wore cloaks of *Shushtari* brocade. As for the horses, ten had bejewelled accoutrements and 20 had plain golden ones. There were 50 *Dailamis* with golden shields, ten of which were ornamented with jewels. The high ranking servants of the State stood by, and outside the portico of the palace there were many palace attenndants and a crowd of infantrymen all armed."

"The court celebrations then took place. The great men of State and holders of high rank came forward. Enormous quantities of largesse were distributed and the prominent people, governors and great men were invited to sit on the dais. The Amir held court, seated on his throne, till morning, when the *Nadims* came in, greeted the Amir, and distributed largesses. Then the Amir rose, mounted and made off to the garden. He changed his robes, rode back and sat down to feast in the splendidly adorned hall. The nobles and great men came forward to the table too. Other tablecloths were spread outside the hall, to one side of the palace, and the *Sarhangan, Khailtashan* and other groups sat down there and began to eat. The musicians struck up and wine flowed like water so that, gradually those who had become drunk left the table. The Amir rose up from the table in a mood of great joy, mounted and rode off to the garden. They organised a splendid *majlis* there similiar to the first. The *Nadims* came along, and they all settled down to drink wine till the evening prayer."[23]

Baihaqi also gives a vivid eye-witness account of the reinstatement of Maimandi, a remarkable man who had served as Mahmud's Wazir and then fallen from grace: "The *Khwaja* (the title given to wazirs at Ghazni) was sent by the Sultan to the robing room to be invested with robes of office. He started dressing at noon after careful consultations with astrologers who determined the auspicious hour. He was dressed in scarlet cloth of Baghdad, embroidered with small flowers and wore a large turban of the finest muslin bordered with delicate lace, a heavy chain and a girdle weighing 1,000 *miskals* studded with turquoise. The captain of the guard sitting at the door presented him, according to custom, a piece of gold, a turban and two enormous turquoises set in a ring. On entering the presence of the Sultan, he was congratulated by the Amir. He kissed the ground in front of the sovereign and presented him with a valuable *bunch* of pearls said to be valued at 10,000 *miskals*." Mahmud gave him the signet of the State engraved with the royal seal "that the people may know that the Khwaja's authority is next to my own". Two days later he took his seat in his office first offering prayers on a fine brocade cloth set with turquoises. Next he called for ink, paper and sand

and wrote a sentence of thanksgiving in Arabic. The whole day, presents of gold, silver, cloth, slaves, pedigreed horses and camels came pouring in. A meticulous list was maintained of these gifts all of which were sent to the Sultan, the Khwaja retaining none for himself. As a gesture of appreciation, the monarch sent back 10,000 pieces of gold, 10 valuable Turkish slaves, five horses from the royal stables and 10 camels.[24]

Notes

1. A.B.M. Habibullah, *The Foudation of Muslim Rule in India*, p. 192.
2. Ibid., p. 194.
3. Ibid., p. 195.
4. I.H. Qureshi, *Administration of the Sultanate of Delhi*, p. 59. Hereinafter referred to as Qureshi.
5. Muhammad Aziz Ahmad, *Political History and Institutions of the Early Turkish Empire of Delhi*, p. 339. Hereinafter referred to as Muhammad Aziz Ahmad.
6. Ibid., p. 56.
7. Elliot and Dowson, *History of India as told by its own Historians*, Vol. II with foreword by M. Habib, pp. 6-7. Hereinafter referred to as Elliot and Dowson.
8. C.E. Bosworth, *The Ghaznavids, Their Empire in Afghanistan and Eastern Iran*, pp. 49-51. Hereinafter referred to as Bosworth.
9. K.A. Nizami, *Some Aspects of Religion and Politics in India during the Thirteenth Century*, pp. 91-96.
10. Qureshi, pp. 59-60.
11. Ibid., p. 63.
12. Ibid., pp. 63-64.
13. Ibid., p. 65.
14. Ibid., p. 65.
15. Ibid., p. 69.
16. Ibid., p. 69.
17. Ibid., pp. 70-71.
18. Ibid., p. 72.
19. Ibid., p. 72.
20. Ibid., p. 73.
21. Muhammad Aziz Ahmad, pp. 337-338.
22. Qureshi, p. 73.
23. Bosworth, pp. 135-137.
24. Elliot & Dowson, Vol. II, pp. 68-72.

4

THE ADMINISTRATIVE, LEGAL AND ECONOMIC SET-UP

THE ADMINISTRATION

The Wazir

Fakhr-i-Mudabbir's Adab-ul-Muluk wa Kifayat-ul-Mamluk says "The kings know well how to lead expeditions, conquer countries and shine in the assembly or the battlefield, but it is the domain of the wazir to make a country prosperous, to accumulate treasures, to appoint officials, to ask for accounts, to arrange the stock-taking of horses, camels, mules and other animals, to assemble and pay the troops and artisans, to keep the people satisfied, to look after the men of piety and of fame and to give them stipends, to take care of the widows and orphans, to provide for the learned, to organise the offices and look after their efficiency, in short to transact the business of the State."[1]

The post being so important, the incumbent had, of necessity, to be a man of wisdom, education and acumen. He had to be well versed in matters of State and to be tactful, diplomatic and charming. He was paid handsomely and maintained an establishment second only to that of the Sultan. His department was known as the diwan-i-wizarat and he was assisted by the Naib-wazir.[2]

The mushrif-i-mumalik and the mustauf-i-mumalik were the accountant-general and auditor-general respectively. The former entered the accounts received from the provinces and the mustauf audited them.[3]

Other Officials

The diwan-i-risalat, dealing with religious matters pertaining to pious foundations, stipends to scholars and holy men, was presided over by the Sadr-us-sudur who was generally also qazi-ul-mumalik and, therefore, controlled the department of justice.

The diwan-i-ard was the office of the arid-i-mumalik who was the controller general of the military department which maintained the roll of horses and men. The arid-i-mumalik himself was inspector general of the forces and through his assistant, enlisted new recruits and fixed their pay.[4]

The diwan-i-insha dealt with royal correspondence and was presided over by the dabir-i-khas assisted by a number of dabirs who had already established a reputation as masters of style in letter writing. Writing was a highly cultivated art and the courts vied with one another in the excellence of their correspondence. The *dabir-i-khas*, the confidential clerk of the State and a repository of State secrets, was one of the most important officials of the State. It was he who wrote the fatahnamahs, the flowery descriptions of victories, which were read out to the people and sent to neighbouring courts. These were collected in volumes like other literary works and served as examples to successive generations of dabirs. The *dabir-i-khas* was often trusted by a Sultan, above even the Wazir and, occasionally, the post could be a stepping stone to the wizarat.[5]

The *barid-i-mumalik* was the head of the State news agency and kept himself well informed about all that was happening in the empire through barids posted in every sub-division who sent him regular newsletters. The *barid* was the confidential agent of the central government to report on all aspects of public administration. He was present at all important functions and review of troops so that the could send his own impressions of the strength and intentions of the governors to the centre. So great was his responsibility, that if it was discovered that he had failed to report a misdeed or some act of gross injustice on the part of a local friend he could be sentenced to death. Only men of proven ability were appointed to the post and were paid well to eliminate the possibility of their being bought over.[6]

This system of information ensured the obedience of the provincial governors to the central authority ,especially if the sovereign was powerful and charismatic enough to deal with nobles inclined to be refractory. It also provided a safeguard against oppression of the people by unscrupulous officials. Qutbuddin Aibak had his own staff of *barids* so that the Delhi Sultanate had its own news network from its very inception. Apart from the barids, the government had a large number of spies who were attached to the household of nobles or wandered the country in the guise of travellers, traders or mendicants. They mixed with common people and got their views and discovered secrets which the barids could not ferret out.[7]

Ambassadors and messengers sent to foreign courts were also instructed to keep their eyes open, to observe conditions, gather information and supply it to the Centre.[8]

Punishment

High officials were richly rewarded and well paid but when they fell from grace the penalty was equally great. Baihaqi describes the fate of a minister accused by his enemies of heresy. He presented the reverse of his glittering shield and was sent to his death clad in nothing but his turban and trousers. His hands clasped together, "his body like shining silver, his face a picture" he calmly faced his doom. Obviously he was much loved, for every man in the crowd gathered to witness his execution wept, and no one would throw the stones that were to be the means of his execution. Mercifully, the executioner spared him the indignity of lapidation by putting a noose round his neck. His mother heard the news much later and weeping, said "What a fortune was my son's. Such a king as Mahmud gave him this world and such a one like Masud the next".[9]

Law & Judiciary

The ministry for religious affairs was under the *Sadr-us-Sudur* who was also qazi-i-mumalik or Chief judge of the empire.[10]

The Sultan was the defender of the Faith, the upholder of Shariah, the law of Islam, and arbiter in disputes of his subjects. He was head of the bureaucracy and commander-in-chief of the forces. In his first capacity, he dispensed justice through the *diwan-i-qada* while, in the latter through the *diwan-i-mazalim.* As commander-in-chief, he himself or his commander, sat as a court-martial to try rebels, though legal opinion about the rights of the case was sought from lawyers.[11]

Personal law

All Muslims were subjected to the law of the Shariah while non-

Muslims were judged according to their own laws in matters of inheritance, marriage etc. This could be tribal or local law or the Hindu Code, depending on the religion or area to which the parties belonged. In matrimonial matters the jurisdiction of the *qazi* extended over the *zimmi*, only when asked for, and even then the judge was obligated to take into account practices pertaining to the party's religion or caste. Jurists thus recognised two systems of law, the *tashrii* and the *ghair tashrii*.[12]

Criminal law

In criminal matters, every one stood on the same footing and was subjected to the *diwan-i-mazalim wa adl*. This body dated back to early Muslim times and, in India, the kings personally heard the complaints of their subjects.They sat surrounded by their bodyguard and officers and received complaints of the public. Supplicants could also present petitions when the Sultan rode out. Ibn Batuta mentions a bell attached to a chain in the palace of Iltutmish that any supplicant could ring and demand justice from the king.

Governors were expected to sit as *mazalim* courts. They were helped by the *diwan* and *qazi*. They also heard complaints against officials. If the parties were dissatisfied with the judgement they could go to civil courts for redress.[13]

Qazis

The whole legal system of administration of religious affairs was under the chief *qazi* who heard appeals from the lower courts and appointed local qazis. Every town of reasonable size had a *qazi* whose responsibilities included management of the property of widows and orphans, the execution of testamentory dispositions and the supervision of *awqaf*. He helped destitute widows to find suitable husbands; dispensed justice, maintained roads and prevented encroachments on thoroughfares or open land. Great importance was attached to the qazi of the capital. Quite often, the Sultan himself invested the incumbent.

The *diwan-i-qaza's* main concern was with civil litigation although it had contacts with the departments of *Siyasat* and *mazalim*. Its head was the Qazi-i-Mumalik who was almost invariably the Sadr-us-Sudur. He was assisted by a Naib.[14]

Amir-i-Dad

It was the duty of the *amir-i-dad* to see that the qazi's decisions were carried out. He enforced the sentence, but if he felt that there had been a miscarriage of justice, he could either draw the *qazi's* attention to the matter or delay its execution until a higher court had looked into it. He was also responsible for the proper maintenance of mosques, bridges and public buildings as well as of the city walls and gates. He also controlled the *kotwal* and the police.[15]

Muhtasib

The Muhtasib was regarded as the guardian of public decency and the protector of the weak against the strong. His duty was to suppress illegal practices and to punish the wrongdoer. However, his jurisdiction extended to cases arising out of clear wrong doing only. In disputed cases, the matter went to the *qazi*. The *muhtasib* saw to it that public prayers were conducted properly; intoxicating liquors and drugs were not manufactured and sold publicly; that no one practised fraud and cheated others; and gambling, illegal marriages and acts of indecency did not take place.

The important difference between the functions of a *muhtasib* and a *qazi* was that the former had spontaneous powers of intervention while the latter could act only when a litigant applied to him. It was the *muhtasib's* duty to protect slaves and servants from mal-treatment and prevent them from being over-worked. School masters who beat their pupils severely were also reprimanded by him. He saw to it that houses likely to collapse were demolished and that no building went up high enough to disturb the neighbour's privacy. In short, he was responsible for the smooth running of civic life in the city. He supervised markets and inspected weights and measures; prevented adulteration of food-stuffs and punished defaulters. He was also responsible for the maintenance of the purity of doctrine and, to this end, kept a sharp eye on preacher and pedagogue to prevent the dissemination of heresy.[16]

Judicial Officers

In the early days of the Sultanate, and even later, the system of local government was hardly touched and the village or caste panchayat carried on its traditional functions taking care not to clash with the Qazi's jurisdiction. Barani mentions a body of customary law which he calls *zabita* followed by the government in dealing with Hindu subjects.[17]

A *qazi-i-lashkar* dispensed justice in the army and administered martial law. Only honest men well-versed in the *Shariah*, were appointed to the post.

Payment to judicial officers, as in the case of others, could be either in cash or revenue assignments.

The *rais-i-bazaar* maintained law and order in markets, supervised commercial dealings, checked dishonesty and punished hoarders and profiteers.

The *Kotwal* maintained law and order in towns and even helped in military defence.[18]

Justice was a primary concern of the Sultans. The Prophet is reported to have said that a moment spent in the dispensation of justice is better than seventy years of devotion. "Dominion can subsist inspite of mischief but it cannot endure with the existence of injustice."[19]

"The Sultanate provided a well-organised department of justice, by making all proceedings public and dividing responsibility and power among different officials, it established an effective system of checks and balances" writes Qureshi.[20]

The Sultans themselves respected the law and even a harsh king like Muhammad bin Tughlak, according to Ibn Batuta, showed humility and appeared before the *Qazi* when complaints were made against him. He accepted the verdict of the court and went so far as to walk to the court and to ask the *Qazi* not to rise when he (the king) entered the court.

Firuz Shah did not hesitate to execute a favourite who was found guilty of murder and ordered a high official to be executed for the murder of an obscure student.[21]

Finance & Currency

The main sources of income to the State were:

1. Tax on agricultural produce called *kharaj* and *ushr*.
2. Jiziyah--the tax levied on Hindus and often on converted Muslims.
3. 1/5 of the booty captured in war.
4. Zakat--a tax on Muslims that could only be spent on specified items.[22]

Revenue

In India, the main revenue had always come from land. All land was classified into ushr and kharaj. Ushri was land that was irrigated by rivers, lakes, springs and wells, and belonged to those who had converted to Islam of their own accord and had been left in possession of their lands. It also applied to all land conquered by force and distributed among Muslim soldiers. The rate charged on ushri land was uniform. Where the crops were irrigated by rain or flood water, and for wild fruit, the growing of which did not require exceptional labour, the revenue was 1/10 of the produce. Where the crops had to be irrigated manually requiring hard work, the rate was 1/20 of the produce.[23] Aibak commanded that all land owned by the Muslims should be regarded as ushri.

Kharaji was land that was irrigated by channels dug or controlled by the State as was the water contained in reservoirs built with public money. The levy on it was 1/5 of the produce. Any ushri land bought by a non-Muslim became Kharaji and was taxed accordingly.[24]

All land conquered by force and not distributed among Muslims but left to its non-Muslim owners, was considered kharaji. If the owner of kharaji land converted to Islam the land remained kharaji and land developed by Muslims using kharaji water also remained kharaji. The demand for kharaji land was adjusted according to the vagaries of the weather.[25]

The importance of agriculture was thus recongnised early on, and even though Muhammad bin Tughlak (1325-1351) is commonly supposed to have been the first monarch to have set up a Ministry of Agriculture called diwan-i-amir-i-kuhi, an amir-i-kuhi had been earlier mentioned under Iltutmish.[26]

Jiziyah

The jiziyah was a poll tax levied by Muslim conquerors on the *zimmis* and *muahids*, allies and protected people. The tax was levied in India for the first time by Muhammad bin Qasim (in the 8th century A.D.) on his conquest of Sind and was imposed at the rates universally recognised in the Muslim world. The Sultans of Delhi assessed this tax in their own currency.

A tax like the jiziyah had been well known in the ancient world and was imposed by Romans on non-Romans. It was also levied in India by the Gaharwar dynasty of Kanauj. Called the it was levied either on

Hindus to protect the kingdom from Muslims or on Muslims who were resident in the kingdom.[27] Even in Tod's days, a poll tax of a rupee per head was levied in certain Rajput States.[28]

The jiziyah was levied, for the first time, by Prophet Muhammad on the Christians of Najran in 8 AH/630 AD and the privileges of the zimmi, the protected people, were thus explained in a message. "To (the Christians of) Najram and the neighbouring territories, the security of God and the pledge of His Prophet are extended for their religion and their property--to the present as well as the absent and others; besides there shall be no interference [with practice of] their faith or other observances; nor any change in their rights or privileges. No bishop shall be removed from his monastery, nor any priest from his priesthood, and they shall continue to enjoy everything great and small as hithertofore; no image or cross shall be destroyed; they shall not oppress or be oppressed."

Thus, once the non-believer agreed to pay the jiziyah he was fully under the protection of the State as far as his religion and place of worship were concerned.[29]

The word jiziyah is an Arabised form of the Persian word, gezit, meaning tax. It was first formulated by ancient Persian king, Nausherwan, who imposed the tax as an alternative to military service. Originally, under a Muslim regime every Muslim could be forced to perform military service but non-Muslims could not be so obliged, since their ideology was recognised as being different, and therefore they could not be expected to be willing to die for a creed at variance from their own. But since, the Muslim soldiers protected the life and property of the non-Muslim, the latter was expected to pay a tax. Moreover, if at any time, the government failed to offer such protection the tax money was returned to the payer. Any non-Muslims voluntarily enlisting as soldiers were exempted from the tax. Women, mendicants, invalids, lunatics and those possessing less than 200 dirhams were also exempted from payment of the tax, the proceeds of which were meant to be spent on maintenance of the army and protection of frontiers. Any surplus was to be spent on public works such as roads and bridges.[30]

Conversion to Islam meant loss of revenue from jiziyah, so the later Caliphs discouraged conversion and in case of converts, the jiziyah money continued to be realised.[31]

There is no clear indication of the nature and imposition of jiziyah in the thirteenth century in India. Perhaps the sheer logistics of the imposition of such a tax deterred the rulers from levying it. The elaborate machinery required for the imposition and collection of the tax on such a large scale could not have been set up so soon after the conquest.

Barani recounts an incident when some of the Ulema went to Iltutmish and demanded the removal of the status of zimmis from the Hindus, listing them as *Kafirs* (since obviously they did not pay the jiziyah). The king asked his *wazir, Nizam-ul-mulk* Junaidi, to give a reply to the demand. The wazir said, "But at the moment, India has been newly conquered and the Muslims are so few that they are like salt (in a large dish)... when in the capital and in the regions and small towns, Muslims are well established and the troops are larger, it will be possible to give Hindus the choice of 'death or Islam'. "[32]

The story, which has not been repeated by any other writer may not be accurate but its basic good sense cannot be doubted. The *wazir* obviously sensed that with too much unwarranted oppression the Hindus could combine and throw out the invaders.

The earliest mention of the jiziyah is by Firoz Khalji (1290-1296) in whose time it appears to have been rather haphazard, and Firoz Tughlak (1351-1388) who consciously levied the tax according to Islamic tenets. He records the realisation of the jiziyah from the Brahmins who had been exempt from it, as a service he had rendered to Islam. He also mentions abolishing jiziyah on those who had embraced Islam, thus suggesting that, earlier, conversion had been no excuse for not paying the tax.[33]

Booty

The proportion of the booty accruing to the exchequer was supposed to be 1/5 of the total amount captured during a campaign. However, no rigid rules seem to have been observed in this respect, and the amount appended depended entirely on the Sultan's whim. According to Firoz Tughlak's remarks, earlier Sultans had retained 4/5 of the booty leaving only 1/5 to the soldier--exactly opposite of the practice prescribed by the law, and in many wars the entire bounty was retained by the royal treasury. With war a constant fact of life, the booty itself thus formed an enormous source of revenue.[34]

Zakat

The *zakat* enjoined by the Quran on every Muslim, was levied at 1/40 the value of merchandise and 5% on horses. The amount was probably spent for upkeep of religious establishments, pensions for the *ulema* and other religious causes. It could be paid in gold, silver, herds and merchandise.[35]

Taxes

The property of a Muslim dying intestate and without heirs belonged entirely to the State while the property of zimmi was, in similar circumstances, handed over to his community.[36] Other income came from taxes levied on houses, orchards, shops, butchers etc. and other old Indian taxes which had been mentioned by Manu as being levied on meat, honey, ghee, perfumes, medicines, liquids, flowers, roots and fruits as well as on leaves, herbs, grass, hides, *rattan* work, earthen pots and stoneware.[37]

Other sources of income were presents to the sovereign and provincial governors.

The taxes were collected directly by the *diwan-i-wazarat* in the khalisah area, that was governed directly by the Centre, and by the *muqti's* revenue department in the provinces.[38]

The expenditure on each department was, more or less, fixed depending on the exigencies of the time and the temperament of the monarch. The Sultans were lavish spenders but the more efficient ones did build up large reserves which could help a descendent in times of need or be depleted by a profligate ruler.[39]

As in so many other things, the conquerors mostly adopted the local coinage, retaining the design and device of the existing coins on the new currency. The *dehliwala*, a coin of mixed metal was first used and later came to be replaced by the *jital*. The bull, horseman and devi of the Hindu coinage with the sovereign's name in Devanagari script continued until the end of the 13th century.[40]

Nelson Wright writes "Iltutmish was a great moneyer. That he established the silver *tankah* and the *billon jital* on a firm footing was in itself a remarkable achievement. The influence of his silver *tankah* may be said to have continued down to the present day. His incorporation of the 32 *ratti* weight standard into his currency scheme was a skilful move which made for both popularity and permanence. Iltutmish may also be credited with extending to India the trans-frontier practice of putting on the *tankah* the name of the mint-town, a practice which was continued in subsequent years by his successors and to a still greater extent, by the Suris and the Mughals. Moreover, he enhanced the importance to be attached to the currency by the complete provision which he made in the copper coinages for the needs of all, even the poorest, his *adls* being found weighing as little as 8 to 10 grams.[41]

Billon was an alloy of silver and bronze. Mixed metal coins were known in India from very early times and when the Muslims came to the country they found a local coinage consisting apart from the gold issues, almost entirely of mixed metal pieces and the practice was incorporated by them in their own currencies.[42]

The word '*tankah*' indicated an Indian weight of silver. With the *Kalimah* in Arabic and the sovereign's name and titles the *tankah* became the standard monetary unit of the Delhi Sultanate. Later, the name of the Caliph was added. The *jital*, towards the end of the 16th century, was worth 1/48 of *tankah*.[43]

The Sultanate currency was so expertly planned and adjusted that it remained steady throughout the century. It was incorporated into the Indian weight standard. Being tri-metallic, the relationship, one to the other, was determined by the intrinsic metal value of the pieces. There were silver *tankahs*, ten of which were equal to one gold *tankah*. There were 1/2 *tankahs*, *fals* or *adl*, *jitals*, 1/2 *fals*, double *jitals*, three *jital* pieces and so on.[44]

Notes

1. I.H. Qureshi, *Administration of the Sultanate of Delhi*, p. 50. Hereinafter referred to as Qureshi.
2. Ibid., p. 84.
3. Ibid., p. 84.
4. Ibid., p. 85.
5. Ibid., pp. 87-88.
6. Ibid., pp. 89-90.
7. Ibid., p. 91.
8. Ibid., p. 92.
9. Elliot & Dowson, *History of India as Told by its Own Historians*, Vol. II, p. 100.
10. Qureshi, p. 157.
11. Ibid., p. 157.
12. A.B.M. Habibullah, *The Foundation of Muslim Rule in India*, p. 271. Hereinafter referred to as Habibullah.
13. Qureshi, p. 159.
14. Ibid., pp. 159-161.
15. Ibid., p. 162.
16. Ibid., pp. 154-169.
17. Barani, *Fatawa-i-Jahandari*, Translated as *The Political Theory of the Delhi Sultanate* by M. Habib and Afsar Umar Salim Khan, p. 126.
18. Ibid., pp. 47-108.
19. Qureshi, p. 162.
20. Ibid., p. 163.
21. Ibid., pp. 163-164.

22. Habibullah, p. 232.
23. Qureshi, p. 101.
24. Ibid., pp. 102-103.
25. Ibid., p. 132.
26. Ibid., p. 128.
27. Ibid., p. 98.
28. James Tod, *Annals and Antiquities of Rajasthan*, edited by William Crooke, p. 1116.
29. K.A. Nizami, *Some Aspects of Religion and Politics in India during the Thirteenth Century*, p. 309.
30. Ibid., pp. 310-311.
31. Ibid., p. 313.
32. Ibid., p. 316.
33. Habibullah, p. 233.
34. Shams Siraj Afif, "Tarikh-i-Firuz Shahi", in Elliot and Dowson, Vol. III, p. 383.
35. Qureshi, p. 95.
36. Ibid., p. 100.
37. Manu, *Dharamsastra*, Vol. VIII, pp. 129-133.
38. Habibullah, p. 235.
39. Qureshi, p. 134,
40. Habibullah, p. 235.
41. Nelson Wright, *The Coinage and Metrology of the Sultans of Delhi*, p. 75.
42. Ibid., p. VII.
43. Habibullah, pp. 236-237.
44. Ibid., p. 240.

5

PROVINCIAL, MILITARY AND FOREIGN AFFAIRS

Iqtas

Iqta and *wilayat* are two words used in the chronicles to indicate a division of the kingdom. The word *iqta*, meaning a portion, appears to have been used in Central Asia from where the Turks adopted it. The holder of the *iqta*, the *muqti*, though subject to control by the sovereign, was allowed considerable latitude in matters of administration and war.[1]

The *siyasat namah* of Nizamulmulk Tusi lays down the following rules for the guidance of the *muqti*. "They (the *muqttis*) should know that their right over the subjects is only to take the rightful amount of money or perquisite (*mal-i-haq*) in a peaceful manner... the life, property and the family of the subject should be immune from any harm, the *muqtis* have no right over them; if the subject desires to make a direct appeal to the Sultan the *muqti* should not prevent him. Every *muqti* who violates these laws should be dismissed and punished... the *muqtis* and *walis* are so many superintendents over them as the king is superintendent over other *muqtis*.... After three or four years the *amils* and the *muqtis* should be transferred so that they may not be too strong."[2]

The *muqti* had his own contingent equipped and maintained out of the revenue of his province, the rest going to the Central Government. However, even though they did enjoy a degree of freedom it does not seem to have been as great as that enjoyed by the fief lords of Europe.

The *muqtis* were appointed by the Sultan and could be transferred at the latter's will. His troops, maintained from part of the revenue collected, could be requisitioned by the Central Government. Although there is no record of revenues being regularly required to be sent to Delhi instances are not wanting to prove that such demands were made. In 1204 Muizuddin directed the *muqti* of Lahore and Multan to despatch the arrears of revenue to enable him to make preparations for his campaign in Trans-oxiana. According to Barani, Muhammad, eldest son of Balban and Viceroy of Sind, used to bring the revenue of his province every year personally to his father. Alauddin *Khalji*, as *muqti* of Kara and Awadh, asked Firoz *Khalji* for permission to utilise the surplus revenue of his province for purchasing horses and employing troops for an advance on Chanderi.

Ghiyasuddin Tughlak directed his newly appointed officers thus -- "If you desire that you may not be taken to task by the *diwan-i-wazarat* (Finance Ministry). . . . You may not be avaricious, take little from the iqta and with this defray your expenses and pay your troops and do not take a single farthing from the pay of the troops."

According to Barani, "Those (*muqtis*) who embezzle the money and tamper with the accounts and exact more than the specified share from the *iqta*, would be punished with chains and imprisonment."[3]

Iqtidars (assignees) differed from *muqtis* in that they had no financial liability to the financial exchequer. They were assigned the revenue of villages as pay for their personal service in the army. *Qazis* and *amir-i-dads* were granted land for non-military service.[4]

Newly acquired territories and fortresses seem to have been directly placed under military officers. Kara on the Ganges, near Prayag, was originally a military command under an amir but later became an *iqta*. Gwalior was always under *an amir*.[5]

There is little information about Muslim peasantry in the early years. Obviously the Muslims preferred the urban to the rural environment. The Hindus, who formed the bulk of the peasantry in most provinces, paid revenue through the village headman called *muqaddam* or *chaudhuri*. Some Hindu chiefs were placed under the *muqti* while others paid money directly to the royal treasury.[6]

The *muqti* generally lived in the province assigned to him but some, especially those placed near the capital, were absentee governors who ruled through *naibs* or deputies. Balban who held the office of *Amir-i-hajib* and *naib-i-mamlikat* which required his constant presence at court must have administered his *iqta* of Hansi through a subordinate. Later when the *iqta* was transferred to the infant son of Mahmud it had, of necessity, to be administered by a *naib*.[7]

The *muqti* was given powers to supervise troops, punish criminals and rebels and guard his territory. Administration of justice and levying of taxes, however, were not within his powers. He was also not allowed to lead prayers or act as spiritual head of the people, that being strictly the Sultan's prerogative. Sometimes, for reasons of distance from the capital (as in the case of Lakhnauti) or for other reasons it became necessary to appoint a powerful man as governor. Such men, naturally, exercised the authority of a semi-independent monarch within their domain. It was they who organised and posted the army and judicial officers, raised taxes, managed the finances and were protectors and defenders of the Faith. The ordinary governors were known as *imarat-i-ammah* while the latter were known as *imarat-i-khassah.* A strong governorship taken by force through a rebellion, was known as *imarat-i-istila.*[8]

Constant vigilance was required by the Centre to combat centrifugal tendencies and to keep ambitious governors under control. The *Taj-ul-maathir* records Aibak's instructions to a governor thus:-

1) To protect and enforce the laws, traditions and regulations;
2) To look after the *ulema*, the warriors and civil officials;
3) To reconcile the people by reducing their dues and introducing measures of prosperity;
4) To increase the produce by extending cultivation;
5) To maintain justice and protect the weak from the tyranny of the strong;
6) To ensure the enforcement of court decisions;
7) To desist from capital punishment;
8) To guard the highways, encourage trade and protect traders.[9]

Hasan Nizami says, "... He (the governor) should take pains to fulfil the expectations of the people; he should exercise the greatest circumspection in military matters; and he should maintain the traditions of benevolence and charity so as to leave a name for eternity.[10]

In every province there was a *Sahib-i-diwan*, also called *Khwaja* who was appointed by the Sultan on the recommendation of the *Wazir*. He was generally an expert accountant and his duty was to maintain account books and submit detailed statements to headquarters. It was on the basis of this that the Central government settled accounts with the *muqti*. His presence provided a check on the authority of the governor.[11]

Communications

Good communications are the lifeline of any State. They were necessary for keeping the Centre informed about happenings in remote areas of the kingdom; to keep the lines open to the capital during campaigns, to feed the troops and to make the imperial will known to governors, bureaucrats and generals.

Roads were very important and one of the main duties of Aibak's governors was to keep them in good repair. Travellers had to be protected from thieves and marauders. For this purpose forts were built at strategic points, the *Kotwals* of which were responsible for keeping the roads open and punishing thieves. Thanas, containing bodies of troops, were also erected.[12]

Ibn Batuta, who came to India in 734 AH/1333 AD was a native of Tangiers and was loaded with riches and honours by Muhammad bin Tughlak. He described his travels within the country giving a good account of parvailing conditions. About the postal system he writes, "The *barid* or post in India is of two kinds. The horse post is called *ulak* and is carried by means of horses belonging to the Sultan stationed at every four miles. The foot post is thus arranged: Each mile is divided into three equal parts, called *dawah*, which signifies 1/3 of a mile. Among the Indians, the mile is called *Kos*. At each 1/3 of a mile there is a village, well populated, outside of which are three tents, in which are men ready to depart. These men gird up their loins and take in their hands a whip, about 2 cubits long, tipped with brass bells. When the runner leaves the village, he holds the letter in one hand and in the other the whip with the bells. He runs with all his strength and when the men in the tents hear the sound of the bells they prepare to receive him. When he arrives, one of them takes the letter and sets off with all speed. He keeps on cracking his whip until he reaches the next *dawah*. Thus the couriers proceed until the letter reaches its destination.

This kind of post is quicker than the horse post and the fruits of Khurasan which are much sought after in India, are often conveyed by this means.... It is by this channel that great prisoners are transported. They are each placed upon a seat which the runners take upon their heads and run. . . ."[13]

Al Umari writing in 1348 states, "Every *Dak Chauki* [postal station] is studded with a mosque where people offer their prayers in congregation. The travellers stay there. There are tanks for supplying water and *bazars* for purchasing food and fodder. For this, no traveller has to carry provisions or tents with him."

One of the aspects of the Sultan's [government] is the drums that have been placed in the *Dak Chaukis* for the transmission of information between the two capitals, Delhi and Qubat-ul-Islam (Deogiri). Whenever an important thing happens in any city or any fort is conquered or besieged, the drums are beaten. As the sound reaches the next station, the drum is beaten there also and in this way, the Sultan, who is far away from the place of action, gets information about the capture or siege of the city.[14]

Foreign Relations

"The intimate contact between India and the outer Asiatic world," remarks Sir Jadunath Sarkar, "which had been established in the early Buddhist age was lost when the new Hindu society was reorganised and set in rigidity like a concrete structure about the 8th century A.D. with the result that India again became self-centred and isolated from the moving world beyond her natural barriers. This touch with the rest of Asia and the nearest parts of Africa was restored by the Muslim conquest at the end of the 12th century."[15]

The Turks, of course, had no intention of shutting themselves up in their new home. The need for maintaining diplomatic relations with neighbours was fully appreciated. The *Adab-ul-Harb wa Shujaat* of Fakhri-i-Mudabbir lays down elaborate qualifications for ambassadors, and charts in detail their functions and duties while on assignment in foreign courts. The ambassador should, of course, be well born but he should also be "... formidable, handsome, eloquent, glib-tongued, pert, of tall stature and graceful so that he may command respect in the eyes of the people. He should be cultured, modest, sedate, lavish, charitable, magnanimous, spendthrift, extravagant to an extent that nothing is too much in his eyes.... The envoy should be such that when he commences a discourse meekly he must close it in a harsh manner and should close it meekly if he has begun it harshly. He should be a 'tearer' and the same time a 'sewer', a 'maker' and a 'burner' simultaneously ... his mouth is the mouth of his master."[16]

All agreements were to be made in writing and both parties should agree to act upon them. These agreements were signed by notables of both sides and read out before both parties.

He also gives a long list of commodities suitable for sending as presents to foreign rulers. These include furs of different kinds; china dishes; elephants, precious stones, expensive textiles such as velvet and silk; scented materials such as amber and musks; slaves, arms, horses etc.[17]

The Army

The army was undoubtedly one of the most, if not the most important arm of the State. The constant danger from the Hindu rulers within the country, and from the Mongols at its borders made it imperative for the Sultan to have an armed body constantly on the alert and ready to take up arms at a moment's notice.

The Ministry of War was called the *diwan-i-ard*. At its head, was the *aris-i-mumalik*, responsible for overseeing all military affairs and recruiting soldiers. Candidates displayed their skill and prowess before him and he fixed their salary and put them on the pay roll. He inspected troops and maintained muster rolls. He was responsible for the preparations of campaigns and the selection of soldiers to participate in them. The commissariat was under him and he was in charge of matters dealing with supply and transport. He also supervised the collection of booty which was divided in front of him. Usually he accompanied the army in battle and maintained a description of each soldier called *huliya*.[18]

Qureshi quotes a description of a review of troops. The *arid*, from a point of vantage saw the left wing, the centre and then the right wing march past him, both cavalry and infantry. The *naqibs* stood by and the *arid* scrutinised the deportment, uniform, arms and horse of each soldier. The *naqibs* had charts for arranging the soldiers in battle array, each soldier having his appointed place.[19]

The cavalry formed the backbone of the army, since on its swiftness and manoeuvrability depended the success of most campaigns. Horses were bought or bred in the royal stables and when the Mongol invasion cut off the supply of foreign horses the Sultans could meet the needs of the army indigenously. It was also considered necessary to provide extra horses so that the cavalry was divided into *sawar* and *do-aspah* i.e. men with a single horse each or two horses for one man.[20]

Foot soldiers were called *payak* and were either slaves or those who wanted employment but could not afford horses. The Sultans provided some of the foot soldiers with horses for the actual fighting but paid them the salaries and allowances of infantry men.[21]

Attached to each army was a *sahib-i-barid-i-lashkar* who was the official news writer and sent reports to the capital.[22]

Composition

The army was composed of many races, care being taken to let no one race dominate the other. From the very beginning, the tribal elements in the army were so balanced that any one of them could, if capably led, gain power. Thus, the Khaljis established a semi-independent kingdom in Bengal where they built up enough power to finally oust the Turkish rulers from Delhi. The *Ghaznavids* gave important posts to Hindus--there were a few nobles with the influence of Tilak, the son of a Hindu barber. Hindu soldiers fought for them against the Seljugs and Aibak employed Hindu cavalry. By and large, the army was so balanced that a powerful ruler would never be totally dependent on any one section.[23]

The muslim army, from very early times, was based on the decimal system. There were commanders of 10,000 horsemen or more, 1,000 horsemen, 100 horsemen or less. The term *sipah-salar*, which later came to denote no more than a centurion, applied in early Sultanate days to the Commander-in-Chief and was proudly displayed by Aibak on his buildings.[24]

Strict discipline was maintained and the orders of a superior had to, under all circumstances, be obeyed promptly. Even during a campaign, damage to crops and property was carefully avoided unless express orders for plunder were given.[25]

Large banners were carried with the army. Qutbuddin Aibak's banners bore the figures of a crescent, a lion or a dragon. On the right hand side was carried a black banner being the Abbasede colour and on the left hand side a red banner, the colour of Ghur.[26]

Aibak established garrisons in various places which were placed under *kotwals*, a corruption of the Hindu term, *Kotpal*, guardian of the fort.[27]

The exact composition of the army is not quite certain but the Sultan's bodyguard, the *jandars*, must have formed its nucleus. There seem to have been 4 parts to the army-- (1) regular soldiers employed by the Sultan, (2) troops maintained by provincial governors, (3) special recruits in times of need, (4) volunteers, especially Muslims, who carried their own arms and fought for only a part of the booty especially during a *jihad*, holy war.[28]

Provincial Forces

The provincial force was the governor's own and its efficiency and maintenance were his concern, the *ariz-i-mamalik* exercising little control over it except when a contingent was called up by the Centre. In that case, it was his duty to check the numbers of men and equipment for any discrepancy between statistics supplied by the local authorities and the numbers actually received at the Centre. The number of the provincial army, the rate of pay etc. do not seem to have been controlled by the Centre nor is there any evidence of troops being transferred from one region to another.[29]

Soldiers received their pay either in cash or kind. They could be allotted pieces of land whose revenue provided them with an income. Out of his pay, the soldier had to provide his own arms and horses and keep both in good trim. It was only after approval of the condition of both that pay could be drawn. Booty money supplemented the salary drawn.[30]

Recruitment

For purposes of recruitment holy men were sent to deliver discourses which would cause people to enlist in the army. For instance, in 1241 when the Mongols besieged Lahore, Minhaj-us-Siraj was directed by the King to exhort the people of the city to join the army and special levies were held to raise troops. Balban on his way to Lakhnauti, stopped in Awadh and enrolled large numbers of men as archers, horesemen and infantrymen.[31]

Troop Formation

The *Adabul Harb* gives a description of troop formation during a battle. On two sides of the *qalb* or *muqaddama* (vanguard) were drawn up the *maisara* (left wing) and the *maimana* (right wing) while a picked body of troops formed the *khalf* or rear, to be used only as a last resort. A special force composed of 400 light cavalry commanded by an *Amir* could be used for swift movement or reconnaissance.[32]

Minhaj gives a most interesting account of a battle between Ala-ud-Din, uncle of Sultan Muizuddin of Ghur and Yamin-ud-Din Bahram Khan for the suzerainty of Ghazni. The latter, hearing of the intentions of Ala-ud-Din to take back the territory from which his family had been ousted, sent word to him saying, "Return again to Ghur, and in thy ancestral possession remain in quietness, for thou will not be able to resist my forces, for I bring elephants [along with me]." To which Ala-ud-Din replied "If thou bringest elephants I will bring the Kharmil . . . ."

When the envoys returned, both armies were marshalled and prepared for battle. Ala-ud-Din called his *Pahalwans* (champions) who were leaders of the army and were famous warriors. Both were named Kharmil--one was Kharmil-i-Sam, father of Nasir-ud-Din, Hussain-i-Kharmil, and the other Kharmil-i-Sam, Banji. He told them of the message he had sent to Bahram Khan and directed each of them to kill an elephant. Minhaj records, "When the battle commenced, both these champions dismounted, fastened up the skirts of their coats of mail and entered the fight. When the elephants of Bahram Shah made a charge, each of those champions attacked an elephant. Getting beneath the armour of the animals, with their poinards, they ripped open the bellies of the elephants. Kharmil-i-Sam, Banji, remained under his elephant and it fell upon him and he and the elephant perished together. Kharmil-i-Sam, Husain brought his elephant to the ground and got away in safety and mounted [his horse] again."[33]

He goes on to describe the battle that followed. "The troops of Ghor have a method, in the practice of fighting on foot, of making a certain article of one fold of raw bullock-hide, over both sides of which they lay cotton and over all draw figured coarse cotton cloth, after the form of a screen [or breast work] and the name of that article of defence is *Karwah*. When the foot soldiers of *Ghor* place this [screen] upon their shoulders, they are completely covered from head to foot by it; and when they close their ranks, they appear like unto a wall, and no missile or arms can take any effect on it , on account of the quantity of cotton with which it is stuffed.

When the engagement was fairly begun, Daulat Shah, son of Behram Shah, with a body of cavalry and an elephant, made a charge. Sultan Ala-ud-Din directed that the foot soldiers should open their rank of *karwahs* in order to allow Daulat Shah to enter with his whole division. They opened their ranks accordingly. When Daulat Shah, with his body of horses and elephant, entered, the infantry closed the breach in their ranks again and completely surrounded the Prince on all sides; and he, with the whole of that body of horse, were martyred and the elephant was brought to the ground and also killed."[34]

Just before the engagement, Ala-ud-Din donned a crimson-coloured satin surcoat over his armour. When asked the reason for this he replied,"For this reason that, in case my body be wounded by arrow, lance or sword, the redness of my blood, by means of crimson surcoat, will not show upon my armour, so that the hearts of my followers may not become dejected."[35]

This was a great consideration for all medieval armies. The king, or the noble leading the battle, had to be visible at all times, in one piece and in control of his faculties. Somehow he was always the focus, the rallying point of all soldiers during the battle. There was no second line of command, and any time the leader was seen to be grievously wounded and fell from his horse, even most winning armies lost heart and fled from the field leaving the opponents in control of the day.

Notes

1. A.B.M. Habibullah, *The Foundation of Muslim Rule in India*, p. 252. Hereinafter referred to as Habibullah.
2. Nizam ul Mulk Tusi, *Syasat Namah*, p. 37.
3. Habibullah quoting Barani, pp. 210-22.
4. Ibid., p. 211.
5. Habibullah, p. 214.
6. Barani, *Tarikh-i-Firoz Shahi* in Elliot and Dowson, Vol. II.
7. Minhaj-us-Siraj, *Tabaqat-i-Nasiri*, p. 277. Hereinafter referred to as Minhaj.
8. I.H. Qureshi, *Administration of the Sultanate of Delhi*, p. 194. Hereinafter referred to as Qureshi.
9. Ibid., p. 198.
10. Ibid., p. 198.
11. Ibid., p. 198.
12. Ibid., pp. 211-214.
13. Elliot & Dowson, *History of India as told by its Own Historians*, Vol. III., pp. 587-588.
14. Shihab-al-Din Al-Umari, *Masalik al-absar fi-mamalik al Ansar: A Fourteenth Century Arab Account of Inida under Sultan Muhammad bin Tughlaq*. pp. 57-58.
15. J.N. Sarkar, *India Through the Ages*. p. 43.
16. Fakhruddin Mubarak Shah, *Adab ul Harb wa Shujaat*, ff 57-59a.
17. Ibid., ff. 59a, 59b.
18. Qureshi, p. 137.
19. Ibid., p. 137.
20. Ibid., p. 141.
21. Ibid., pp. 143-144.
22. Ibid., p. 151.
23. Ibid., pp. 151-152.
24. Ibid., p. 153.
25. Ibid., p. 154.
26. Ibid., p. 150.
27. Ibid., p. 150.
28. Habibullah, p. 217.
29. Ibid., p. 218.
30. Ibid., pp. 220-221.

31. Minhaj, pp. 195, 317.
32. Habibullah, p. 222.
33. Minhaj, pp. 350-352.
34. Ibid., pp. 352-353.
35. Ibid., p. 352.

6

DELHI

The foundations of Delhi are supposed to have been laid by Yudhishthira, the eldest of the five Pandava brothers, the heroes of the great epic, the Mahabharata, although, of course, no historical records exist of either its founding or growth. It was named Inderprastha and later, under Raja Dehlu, it came to be called Delhi. The two dates for this mentioned by Sir Sayyid Ahmed Khan are approximately 1450 B.C. and 340 B.C.[1] Although he mentions the names of 141 rulers before Rai Pithora, from whom the Muslims wrested the city, evidently it was not an important enough place to be mentioned by travellers and historians. Neither travellers of the pre-Christian era like Nearchus and Megasthenes, nor later one like Cosmos Indicoplenstes, Fa Hien, Hieun Tsang have mentioned Delhi. It came into the limelight when Tomar Rajputs occupied the area in AD 736 and made the city their capital. In the 10th century, Suraj Pal, the Tomar King, built a circular reservoir and a temple near it, in a rocky area 5 Km. south of the city. This spot is now known as Suraj Kund.

The so called "seven cities" of Delhi are basically concentrated in three main areas of urban density in which the succesive citadels were built in medieval times. Raja Anangpal of the Tomar Rajput Dynasty is ascribed by legend to have been the founder of Delhi having moved his capital from Surajkund to Lalkot which had at its entrance two stone lions which were meant apparently to guard the gateway. Any citizen, in distress could ring a bell to have his grievance heard and appeal for justice.

It is connected with Indraprastha, the oldest site in the city which is linked to Purana Kila (Old fort built by Sher Shah Suri who was defeated by Humayun). Indraprastha was one of the five parts or places around which the city was built-these being Kurukshetra, Panipat, Sonepat,

Tilpat and Baghpat. [2]

The Lal kot was built around A.D. 1060. The Tomars were replaced by Chauhans in the twelfth century whose last ruler Prithvi Raj III or Rai Pithora called it Qila Rai Pithora. He enlarged the fortified area of Lal kot and surrounded it with massive walls and ramparts.[3] However, he lost the battle and with his death at Tarain and the cpature of the Qila by Shahab-ud-din Ghori (Mohhamed of Ghor) as his capital, the history of Delhi emerges from the folklore into the clear light of recorded history.[4]

Although the interest in Delhi could not be said to be specially inspired by its great antiquity it can be compared with the great cities of world whose chronicles are virtually unbroken and well documented. No matter what dynasty ruled the empire, Delhi remained its centre and seat. Unlike other places the various cities of Delhi were not re-built in the same place. But were just a few kilometers removed from each other. This can be explained by the fact that the area in which Delhi is situated is of vital importance. It commands the plains of Hindustan and almost of the sub-continent at large. It made possible the contingencies of both maintaining a firm internal control and strong external defence. Its dominance of the world's one of the largest alluvial plains all the way to the Bay of Bengal and an extension of military forts, north and westwards beyond the Khaibar to Kabul provided a certain careful balance of resources which Delhi provided.

As Muslim incursion and subsequent rule spread over north India, the empire being built required a centre of control from where defence of the realm and suppression of rebellion could be quick, decisive and fast. Central Asian empire of Mahmud required 'Gazmi' in Afghanistan as central to the control. Subsequently as the muslim rule spread eastward into the subcontinent, Lahore became the next focal point. Later with Iltutmish conquering Lakhnauti and Gwalior, it was natural for him to choose Delhi as his capital.

In the earlier years a position of strategic strength was of great importance. The position had to be strongly defensible in its own immediate perimeters. The Delhi triangle with its immediate proximaty both to the ridge of the Aravali Hills and the strongly flowing currents of the Yamuna possessed just what was necessary. The water promised a reliable supply for drinking, irrigation and commerce. In the hinterland deserts of Rajasthan was available unlimited amount of redstone building material.

Secondly it had to be remembered that Delhi could not be conveniently or easily outflanked. No army could afford to simply pass it by or leave a strongly and powerfully fortified Delhi in its rear. The risks of the cut of communication and loss of logistic support were too great. Situated as it was between the Aravali Hills and Rajasthan desert of the south and encroaching foothills of the great mountain ranges of the north it commanded a corridor between the Punjab and Hindustan proper. Thus an imperial ruler could use the territory as a crucial piovt on which to turn both his sway and survival.

Finally according to certain writers there is a certain prestige and mystique - the magic of repeated success. Once a city had been established here and a tradition of continuous strength and success established, it began to gather a kind of hallowed reputation. Thus whoever ruled from Delhi could be seen as ruler of India only if his citadel was fixed in Delhi.

Shihabuddin Ghori captured the fort of Rai Pithora and established his capital there. The imperial sway of the Sultanate of Delhi inexorably began to spread its shadow of authority across the sub-continent, being repeatedly built six times in proximity of each other.

However, Rai Pithora never ruled from Delhi. His seat of government was Ajmer. It was the Turks who, realising the strategic value of Delhi, guarded as it was by the Aravali range on one side and commanding the Indo-gangetic plain on the other, made it the capital of what was to become a vast empire. The citadel Lal Kot was obviously very strong and well fortified, while that built by Rai Pithora was weaker although larger. The conquest of the latter could not, according to Cunningham, be called the conquest of Delhi while Lal Kot held out.

The fort had 9 gates and was surrounded by a deep moat in which water from the surrounding jungles was poured so that it was never dry. The Muslims are said to have entered through a gate which they called the Ghaznin Gate. Sir Sayyid admits that he does not know what the previous name of the gate was.[5] However, Cunningham interprets this as stating, that this gate was so called before the entry of the Muslims and asserts that they entered through the Ranjit Gate. His argument is that the strengthening of the gate by a double line of works and by 3 separate out-works immediately in front of the gateway itself shows that this must have been considered the weakest point of the fortress and therefore, it was most likely to have been attacked. The Muslims, after entering the citadel, strengthened the works for their own security. He points out that Iltutmish did exactly the same 40 years later in Gwalior. Having gained entrance to the fortress by the ravine on the west side he immediately closed it by a massive wall so that his enemies could not take advantage of the same weak point.[6]

How Delhi got its name is not a matter of historical record, but is reported by historians as heresay with slight variations. Says Ferishta, "Dehlu is said to have been a prince of uncommon bravery and generosity; benevolent towards men and devoted to the service of God. The most remarkable transaction of his reign is the building of the city of Delhi which derives its name from its founder, Dehlu".[7]

According to Cunningham, the Brahmin tradition is that the iron pillar which stands near the base of Qutab was erected in the 6th century after the stars had pointed out the auspicious moment. It went so deep that it punctured the head of serpent god, *Sheshnag*, who supports the earth. The priests told the Raja that his kingdom would last forever if he did not interfere with the pillar, but the raja's curiosity got the better of him and he had it dug only to find its base covered with blood. He put down the pillar again but this time it missed the serpent's head and remained unsteady. Therefore, the place was called Dhilli (unsteady). Shortly after this, the Muslims made the city their capital and no Hindu has reigned there since (until this century), although the pillar has remained firmly planted.[8]

There is also a controversy about the origin of the Qutab Minar. Thomas Seymour Burt attributes it to the pre-Muslim period, on the ground that it bears inscriptions in the Devnagari script. He contends that the Muslims tried to erect a similar structure in a parallel line with the first but that it was of much inferior material and smaller stones irregularly shaped which collapsed in a short time. He also points to the curving staircase as being an example of Hindu architecture. He declares himself unconvinced that the arabesque design on the outside makes it the work of the Muslim conquerors.[9]

W.H. Sleeman, on the other hand, ascribes it to the Muslims on the ground that nothing similar to it exists in Hindu buildings anywhere in India. He states that the slope of the tower is characteristic of Pathan architecture and points out that the Hindu ruins around Qutab are totally different. According to him, the second minar was abandoned after being raised to about 30 feet because of an error in calculation--the base was too wide and was rising with too small a dimunition of circumference and much more perpendicular than planned. He is of the opinion, that if Shamsuddin had lived longer he would have completed the second tower but because of the turmoil following his death it was never reconstructed and was allowed to fall into decay. Thus the Quwwat-ul-Islam mosque was left with only one tower and remained intact until the time of Timur's invasion at the end of the 14th century. Timur was so impressed with it that he took back a model of it with him to Samarqand together with all the masons he could find in Delhi and is said to have built a mosque on the same plan before he set out to conquer Syria.[10]

Delhi as the capital of Sultanate dates from the reign of Shams-ud-din Iltutmish (A.D 1211-36). Originally Lahore, traditionally the administrative centre of Indian provinces had been the capital of Muslim India. But several years elapsed before Iltutmish was to definitely occupy Lahore and the Western Punjab. Mongol pressure (they took and sacked Lahore in A.D. 1251) contributed to a great extent in the primacy of Delhi and greatly increased the population of the city - owing to the influx of refugees.

The systematic destruction, pillage and sacking of the cities of the Middle East by Mongols left Delhi as the largest and most famous city in the area, dominated by Muslims. It has been described by historians as being the equal of Cairo and Baghdad.

Whatever its origins, the Qutab Minar remained the heart of the first Muslim capital of Delhi. Officers and merchants lived in 3 or 4 storeyed buildings, the latter using the lower storeys for transaction of business. The poor lived in mud huts with thatched roofs. The *Sarais* or inns, which accommodated the travellers were composed of a series of rooms going onto a verandah, *dalan*, built around a central quadrangle.[11]

There is very little contemporary description of early Delhi except for a short passage by Minhaj who says "Towards men of various sorts and degrees, *kazis*, *Imams*, *muftis* and the like, and to *darweshes* and monks, landowners and farmers, travellers from great cities his (Iltutmish's) benefactions were universal . . . and people from various parts of the world he gathered at the capital city of Dihli, which is the seat of the government of Hindustan, and the centre of the circle of Islam, the sanctuary of the mandates and inhibitions of the law, the kernel of the Muhammadi religion. . . . This city, through the number of the grants and unbounded munificence of that pious monarch became the retreat and resting place for the learned, the virtuous and the excellent of the various parts of the world; and those who, by the mercy of God, the most High, escaped from the toils of the calamities sustained by the provinces and cities of Ajam and the misfortunes carved by the [eruption of the] infidel Mughals, made the capital--the asylum of the universe--of that sovereign their asylum, refuge, resting place and point of safety. . . ."[12]

We have to resort to accounts of later writers and travellers to assess the early history of the city which laid the foundation for later growth.

The pattern of Indian cities had been set much earlier. Kautilya's Arthasastra gives precise instructions for the building of forts (naturally all ancient and medieval cities were fortified) which should be situated on an island in the middle of a river; a plain surrounded by low ground, a rocky tract or at the confluence of rivers. They were to be surrounded by moats and ramparts on which thorny and poisonous bushes were planted. Outside the ramparts passages for movement should be closed by forming obstructions such as pits, instruments made from wreaths of thorns, dogs' teeth etc. They should have 12 gates. Inside, would be king's palaces, houses for ministers, priests, high officials and the general public. Each community was to have its special quarter e.g. merchants trading in perfumes, garlands, grains and liquids would be placed on the eastern side together with expert artisans. Manufacturers of threads of all kinds such as worsted and cotton, bamboo mats, skins, armour, gloves, weapons etc. were to be located on the western side. Government departments would also have their allotted quarter. for instance, the treasury and accounts offices would be situated on sites south by east while the superintendents of the city, of commerce and of the army would be located to the east. Here also would live prostitutes, musicians, and merchants trading in cooked rice, liquor and meat. All these directions would be in relation to king's palace which would be situated in the centre of the city.

Widths of various roads were also specified. Chariot roads, royal roads, country paths and pasture grounds would be 4 *dandas* (24 feet) in width while roads leading to burial or cremation grounds and military stations would be 8 *dandas* in width.

There would be a water well for every ten houses.

Provisions such as oils, grains, sugar, medicinal supplies, dried and fresh vegetables and other necessities such as skins, weapons, armour, strong timber, poison, bamboo and garments etc. were to be stored in such quantities as to last for many years. Old commodities were to be replaced by new when received.[13]

This pattern of the cities, especially of placing each trade in a particular street or area, has continued with some variation until this century. Early Delhi, therefore, must have been planned on the same lines. This is borne out by travellers' descriptions.

Ibn Batuta, a native of Tangiers, who visited India in the 1st quarter of the 14th century describes Delhi thus "The wall which surrounds Delhi [this was Jahanpanah, the third city built by Muslims] has no equal. It is eleven cubits thick. Chambers are constructed in it which are occupied by the night watch and the persons charged with the care of the gates. In these chambers also there are stores of provisions called *ambar*, magazines of the munitions of war and others in which are kept *mangonels raadas* [thunderers--a machine employed in sieges]. Grains keep in these chambers without change or least deterioration. I saw some rice taken out of one of these magazines; it was black in colour but good to the taste. I also saw some millet taken out. All these had been stored by Sultan Balban 90 years before. Horse and foot can pass inside this wall from one end of the city to the other. Windows to give light have been opened in it on the outside towards the city. . . .''[14]

He continues ''The city has 28 gates. Their name for gate is darwaza''. These were named after cities like Ghazna, or a man called Najib or after the grain market which was located off the gate. Outside the Ghazna gate, were the cemeteries full of beautiful domed pavilions and planted with flowering shrubs and trees. Says he ''in that country there are flowers in bloom at every season of the year.''[15]

Al-Umari who never visited Delhi but who, having heard of its renown, enquired about it from a visitor. Writing in 1348 he states, ''... he told me that it comprises different cities, every one bears its own peculiar name but all of them combined together are called Delhi. It is extensive in length and breadth and has a circumference of 40 miles ... There are 1,000 *madrasahs* in Delhi, one of which is for the *Shafites* and the rest for the *Hanafites*.''[16]

Coming as they did from the high ranges of the Afghan mountains, the scarcity of water and the heat of Delhi must have been the greatest trial for the Turks. They sought to provide themselves drinking and bathing water and refuge from the blistering summer heat. Ibn Batuta reports, ''Outside Dihli is the large reservoir named after the Sultan Shams Al-Din Lalmish (Iltutmish) from which the inhabitants of the city draw their drinking water. It lies close to the *musalla* [i.e. outside the Ghazna gate]. Its contents are collected from rain water and it is about 2 miles in length and by half that in breadth. Its western side, in the direction of the *musalla*, is constructed with stones and is posed like a series of terraces one above the other, and beneath each terrace are steps leading down to the water. Beside each terrace there is a stone pavilion containing seats for those who have come out to visit the place and to enjoy its attractions. In the centre of the tank there is a great pavilion built of dressed stones, two storeys high. When the reservoir is filled with water it can be reached only in boats, but when the water is low the people go into it. Inside is a mosque, and at most times it is occupied by poor brethren devoted to the service of God and placing their trust in him [i.e. dependent on charity]. When the water dries up the sides of the reservoir they sow sugarcanes, gherkins, cucumbers and green and yellow melons, the latter are very sweet but of small size."[17]

Al-Umari relates that the water in the city was provided by wells which were only 7 cubits deep and were operated by Persian wheels. Drinking water was collected in huge reservoirs. There were many hamams (Baths) in the city. Delhi was surrounded on 3 sides by gardens set in straight line, each one stretching to the extent of 12 miles. The western side was without gardens because of the Aravalli range.[18]

The sufficiency of water was a recurring pre-occupation with the rulers of Delhi. The river also brought agricultural and commercial benefit providing lush harvest and enough food for the population.

In view of this obsession and need for water, the city inexorably moved towards the river Yumana (Jamuna) until Ferozshah Kotla reached its banks. "It was, therefore, natural that a tendency should emerge to shift towards the Yumana river. A suburb first developed at Gayaspur whose name suggests its settlement during the regin of Sultan Ghayasuddin Balban. Since Sufi Saint Shaikh Nizamuddin established his *Jammat Khana* in this suburb, the present Dargha Nizamuddin fixes its site pretty well. Quite obviously it owed its settlement to its being near the bank of the river which just below here takes a turning towards the East; the point was thus nearest the then city of Delhi while being close to the river. Still the distance between the Qutb Minar and Dargah Nizamuddin is about seven miles in a strainght line."[19]

Society

The aristocracy was composed of emigrants--Turks, Persians and Afghans. Few converted Muslims ever reached position of eminence. The Mongol storm, that had destroyed so many kingdoms, brought a flood of mixed nationalities of varying degrees of talent to the court of Delhi which had managed to remain heretofore untouched. Balban claimed that 15 sovereigns from various Middle Eastern kingdoms had found asylum at his court. The Indian Turk considered himself very special because of his escape from the holocaust. However, this uniqueness could not last very long. Inter-marriage mixed blood lines brought local converts to the fore when Imadul Mulk Rawat, a Rajput convert as his name signifies, became *ariz* at Balban's court.[20]

The Turks were mostly *ahl-il-saif*, men of the sword, while literary men, the *ahl-i-qalam*, mere mostly non-Turkish foreigners. The latter formed the ranks of the bureaucracy and held posts of *dabir*, *khatib*, *wazir* and so on. Natives, both Hindu and Muslim worked at lower level clerical and other jobs.

The most influential among the *ahl-i-qalam* or men of letters were, naturally, the ecclesiastics who formed, with *umara*, the nobles, the highest rank of Muslim society. They controlled the educational institutions and discouraged unorthodox thought and learning likely to undermine their position. The only people beyond their pale of influence were the *sufis*, the mystics. Between the two, there was no love lost since one represented established authority, while the other symbolised revolt from dogma. Because of their popular appeal, the mystics could not be easily suppressed and were treated with respect by King and pauper alike.Their ability to rouse the people to a height of frenzy, and thus pose a real danger to state authority, made it necessary to keep them placated.[21]

Among the *ahl-i-saif*, military rank determined social position. The first rank was that of *Amir*, next *Malik* and then *Khan*. The last was held by adult princes of the blood and such of the Turkish *maliks* as were especially honoured by the King. It was also part of the distinction enjoyed by provincial governors. Aibak and Iltutmish never recieved this rank probably because of their meteoric rise to the throne. Only Balban seems to have passed through this rank. The title *Ulugh Khan* (great Khan), second only to that of the King was, naturally, held by one person at a time.[22]

Below the crust of the elite came the common people, the *awam-o-khalq*, artisans, masons, merchants, shopkeepers etc. The really rich merchants, the *tajir* and the *malik-ut-tajir* could be admitted into the fold of nobility depending on their wealth and personal graces. This was true of both Hindus and Muslims. Barani complains about the many Hindu bankers and merchants whose sumptuous establishments outshone those of the Muslims.[23]

Education and culture were at high premium, and even though the unsettled conditions were never conducive to the production of great literature, the tradition of learning did continue under the Sultans. Muslims having always been patrons of learning one of the first institutions set up in a newly conquered place was commonly a *madrasah*, a school, while mosques were places where primary education was imparted. Private and state endowed institutions flourished simultaneously. Iltutmish founded a college at Delhi named after his eldest son, Nasiruddin, and another at Multan called the *Firozi Madrasah.* Both were richly endowed. Barani speaks of a large number of eminent professors teaching in colleges all over the country.[24]

Scholars came up with proper certificates listing their personal qualifications. Colleges were set up by the government and private donors and many teachers set up their own establishments. Poor students who came from smaller towns received charity which helped them pursue their studies.[25]

Barani gives a list of poets, theologians, lawyers, historians and masters of calligraphy in every reign.Nuruddin Muhammad Aufi (liter ary historian), Fakhruddin Mubarak Shah (political theorist), Hasan Nizami and Minhaj Jurjani (chroniclers), along with a host of others, made vital contributions in their special fields. In the Renaissance tradition of Europe, each of these literary men was accomplished in many fields. Badruddin Damashqi and Husamuddin Marikla were great physicians. Hamiduddin, an equally great physician, was also well versed in mathematics and astronomy.[26]

The main interest of the Indian Muslim lay in *tasawwuf* (mysticism), *hadiths* (traditions of the Prophet), *fiqh* (jurisprudence) and *tafsir* (exegesis). Within these limited forms the standard of scholarship was fairly high, and frank and critical opinions were freely expressed about the works done on various classical authorities. Extensive work was done on various aspects of Muslim tradition, philosophy and jurisprudence. However, the work was not original, certainly in the 13th century, it was a restatement or summarisation of work already done by scholars abroad.

The first literary work to be derived from Indian tradition was written by Abdur Rahman, son of Mir Hasan, who lived in Multan. Titled *Sandesarasaka,* it is a poetical romance in the *Apabhramsa* language. The Indianisation of Muslim letters started with Amir Khusrau. This great poet, writer and mystic wrote both poetry and prose that could compare favourably with that of the great Persian poets such as Hafiz and Sa'adi. In certain poems, however, he mixed highly literary Persian with the dialect spoken by the common Indian without in any way bringing down the standard of either content or style. An accomplished musician himself, Amir Khusrau also invented new *ragas* and instruments to enrich the Indian musical tradition. The work was mostly in Persian. There is no record of any important work being produced in Turki in India.

Poetry was an art practised by all. No chronicle is complete without reproduction of vast quantities of poetry in praise of King, or to illustrate certain points, or in honour of an event, or even to castigate kings on certain actions. Hasan Sijzi and Rukn Muhmerah of Badaun are two of the great poetic names of the period.

The city was obviously a teeming, noisy metropolis where necessities, luxuries, vices and virtues of all kinds were available. There was a thriving trade in girls since prostitution was regarded as much of a trade as any other. "For the purpose of offering them to the Sultan's services," writes Barani, "well-known reprobates and old, wicked procuresses had trained up young girls with beauty, slimness, grace and allure, bold, brunettes and shameless--to sing melodiously, to strike the rubab, to recite *ghazals* and to engage in repartees and to play nord and chess. These courtesans, everyone of whom was a danger to cities and kingdoms, were brought up with expensive care. Even before their breasts could ripen to womanhood, they were taught riding, polo-playing and wielding the lance with thousands of accomplishments and graces. Every alluring art and trick that induced the Muslim ascetic to put on the Brahman's thread and drag the mystic to the tavern was taught to them. Indian boys of graceful stature and girls of remarkable looks were taught to sing in Persian and then dressed in robes of brocade; they were trained in courtesies, customs and manners of the court. The ears of handsome boys were pierced for pearl earrings; beautiful young slave girls were decked like brides. And (along with them) there were expert musicians and reciters of the praises of the Sultan in Hindi and Persian, in prose and verse; and also jokers and buffoons (*bhands*), who with one joke could incite the sorrow-hearted to hilarious laughter, and the joyous hearted to such fits that they could not hold their sides from laughing. All these in the hope of Sultan's favour came from far-off places. And the spirit distillers of Koil (Aligarh) and Meerut brought flagons of scented spirits that were 2 or 3 years old."[27]

Writes Al-Umari, "... All of my informers related that the price of a slave girl for service in Delhi does not exceed eight tankas. The girls who are fit for both service and cohabitation cost fifteen tankas... Inspite of this cheapness there are in India such concubines who cost 20,000 tankas or even more. . . . All the informers told me, without exception, that the reason [for this] was the grace of her deportment and the refinement of her manners. Many of the slave girls of this type know the Quran by heart, can write, can recite verses, relate stories and play on the Sitar. They also make display of their ability in the games of chausar and chess. . . ."[28]

Amir Khusrau, the great poet, who was also a mystic and courtier of late 13th and early 14th century wrote, about Delhi nostalgically "Oh Delhi and its young beauties with turbans placed roguishly awry on their heads! They stroll along while in their wake follow their lovers with bloody tears flowing from their eyes. These saucy young Hindus make the Mussalmans sun-worshippers."[29]

Amir Khusrau was extremely proud of being India-born. He lists a number of arguments praising India above other countries. One of these, he says, "is our sweet music, the fire of which keeps the heart and pulse ablaze. The music attracts artists from far and near. They rush to learn it. But it is so difficult and delicate that even 30 to 40 years' stay does not suffice for a foreigner to learn to produce even a light Indian tune. . . . Indian tunes can hypnotise the beautiful spotted deer so much that it does not fear the arrow piercing its heart. The Arab can only intoxicate the camel to follow his tune and go on but the Indian can hunt down the deer with the help of his music."[30]

He writes with great emotion of a great singer of his time. "In our code of exercising preferences and affording patronage, there is a leading clause that whoever leads in any sphere of this fine art [of chamber music] should get his/her dues to such an extent that he/she wishes for no more. Accordingly, therefore, the blessed bird of the auspicious assembly, the Darling of the Realm, the GEM OF A COMPANY, TURMATI KHATUN . . . whenever she wields her CHANG the bird of paradise sings for her, and whenever she sings herself the cuckoos hold their breath . . . and even MUHAMMAD SHAH comes back to life. . . . In the exclusive CONCERT HALLS of the élite she has often unfolded apart intricate SHO'BAS, lying at such imperceptible intervals as one petal from another in (a) rosebud. . . . This VENUS OF EARTH weaves the TWELVE PARDAS into FIVE [fingers] as if sorting out the threads of the finest Chinese silk. . . ."

"She was entrusted with the duties of Amir-i-Murtabin and became so famous that Irani and Turkish Ustads became her disciples. She was a remarkable singer who sang both in the festive parties of the Sultan and "the SECRET SITTINGS OF OURS, the picked ones, from among the great masters of song and music assembled and performed-- may they be graced with forgiveness (as) they are people whose MUSIC may even make the DAY OF JUDGEMENT stand by, and the people around bereft of their senses. . . . of COURSE they sing and play with FIXED PRINCIPLES OF KNOWLEDGE THROUGH ART. But we who are the instruments of organised state are moved by a DIFFERENT PRINCIPLE. Our reward lies in the SKILL OF OUR HANDS AND THROAT; the hands which extend not but before the resonance bowl of our own RUBAB & BARBAT, the throat which does not share any one else's breath but of our own FLUTE.''[31]

The last, of course, is a reference to the mystic importance of music which is a help to the intensification of spiritual and mystical experiences.

The sound of music thus formed an integral part of the nights of Delhi. With women and music, wine formed the third line of the triangle. Almost all the kings were lovers of wine. Occasionally, in a fit of remorse or as self-denial for the success of some project they would renounce liquor and force their subjects to do likewise, but the venture met with little success and was soon abandoned. When Sultan Shah, Khwarazm Shah, began to put pressure on Ghur Ghiyasuddin, brother of Muizuddin Muhammad Ghuri, foreswore liquor and, according to Minhaj, ''devoted himself to rectitude and goodness.'' An emissary of Khwarazm Shah was entertained at a lavish banquet where he was plied with wine so that he would become inebriated enough to reveal the intentions and plans of his master. The *Amirs* and *Maliks* of Ghur also drank wine but the Sultan had a flask filled with sweet pomegranate juice placed at his side. When the time came to drink toasts, his goblet would be refilled from the same flask and presented to him.[32]

Barani records that Alauddin Khalji prohibited wine drinking and wine selling. Vintrers and wine sellers were turned out of the city and all the china and glass vessels of the royal banqueting hall were broken and piled in a heap outside a city gate while all the wine in the cellars was poured out in such huge quantities that it produced mud and mire as in the rainy season. But soon wine, placed in leather bottles and hidden in loads of hay, firewood etc. was reaching the drinkers in large quantities. The harsh penalty for being caught did not deter the earnest drinker and the Sultan was forced to compromise to the extent of allowing private distillation of liquor and drinking in homes provided no drinking parties were held.

The taverns and brothels disturbed citizens who appealed to the authorities to control the noise. One such petition, quoted by Amir Khusrau, says ''The life of humble petitioner, who had been pretty uncomfortable owing to loud all night prayers of the mystics living on either side of his house, had finally become quite unbearable due to the opening of a tavern on the opposite side of the street, with a grocer boy thrown in to enliven the social landscape and help the sale.''[33]

Gambling (*gammarbazi*) and chess (*shatranj*) were other means of entertainment, and hunting, polo (*chaughan*) and wrestling (*kushti*) provided men with exercise.[34]

The population of Delhi was truly cosmopolitan with people of many different nationalities rubbing shoulders with the local people. The roads were full of pedestrians, riders and palanquins.[35]

Visitors were accommodated in the above mentioned inns and serais but important visitors received special treatment. Ibn Batuta describes the hospitality accorded to him. "On arrival at the mansion which had been prepared for my occupation, I found in it everything that was required in the way of furniture, carpets, mats, vessels and bed. Their beds in India are light and one of them can be carried by a single person; every person when travelling has to transport his own bed, which his slave boy carries on his head. It consists of four conical legs with four crosspieces of wood on which braids of silk or cotton are woven. When one lies down on it there is nothing needed to make it pliable, for it is pliable of itself. Along with the bed they brought two mattresses and pillows and a coverlet all made of silk. Their custom is to use white slips made of linen or cotton as cover for the mattress, so that when they become dirty they wash the slips while the bedding inside is kept clean. That night they came with two men, one of them the miller, whom they call the *Kharras*, the other the butcher whom they call the *qassab*. They told us to take from the one so much the exact weights I do not remember now. It is their custom that the meat which they give is equal to the weight of the flour and this which we have described was the hospitality gift of the Sultan's mother. Later on, there was delivered to us the hospitality gift of the Sultan."[36]

The large population demanded various amenities and Al-Umari records, " There are about 70 hospitals (*bimaristans*). Here *Bimaristan* is called *Dar-ul-Shafa*. Besides there are 2,000 *khanqahs* and serais (hospices and inns) in Delhi and its suburbs. There are huge buildings, extensive bazars and numerous hamams (Baths) in the city."[37]

Food supply had to be maintained in a regular manner and at reasonable prices. The highways had to be kept free of robbers and the traveller had to protect himself where government writ did not run. Though the towns were well-run and prospered industrially and commercially, the countryside was in a state of organised chaos. During the time of Iltutmish, the central government was sufficiently strong to control the intermediaries, obviously Hindus, through whom it had, perforce, to deal with the rural population. Whenever the central power weakened, these intermediaries usurped a great deal of power to themselves. When they agreed to pay the revenue, says Habib "It was with a clear mental reservation that they would pay nothing unless compelled to do so at the point of the sword...." Robber barons freely looted grain caravans and other raw materials being brought to the cities for industries. The government set up its own forts along the highway, and merchants travelled in caravans.

Prices of commodities naturally depended on their availability and the city lived in constant fear of regrating (*ihtikar*) of grain for, obviously, merchants were always ready to raise prices not only when they had to pay highly to the wholesaler, but also when they sensed a desperate need in the purchaser. The Turks could only sporadically cope with these problems, and it was not until Alauddin Khalji came to the throne that order was brought to the countryside with the imposition of a regular administrative system. This was so spectaculary successful, that Barani states that the price of grain was fixed and so rigidly enforced that it "never rose one dang, whether the rains were abundant or scanty. This unvarying price of grain in the markets was looked upon as one of the wonders of the time."

In spite of the difficulties of travel and transport, the city was brimming with goods and services of all kinds. Amir Khusrau wrote that everything was available in Delhi, even '*Shir-i-murgh*' (milk of birds).

Piety is an integral part of religion but so is festivity. In Delhi the *masjid* (mosque), the *madrasah* (school and college), the *maqbara* (tomb) and the *khanqah* (hospice) were all centres of religious activity. The mosques, where congregational prayers were offered, doubled as schools and colleges and were the centres of a number of ceremonies connected with marriage, circumcision, naming ceremonies of children and so on.[38]

Mausoleums were centres of brisk activity. Ibn Batuta records that 460 persons were employed at the tomb of Sultan Mubarak Qutab Shah to perform different services.

The fact that Firoz Tughlak forbade the decoration of walls with representation of living objects is a clear indication of the fact that such representation had existed earlier.

But then anyone visiting the Qutab Minar can see carved figures on the columns of the buildings surrounding it. Mahmud of Ghazni may have destroyed the great idol of Somnath but he carried away many of the lesser idols to decorate his palace. Whether this was done as a symbol of victory or because he appreciated the aesthetic qualities of the sculptures is not quite clear.[39]

Money-lending, commerce in horses, clothes, grain, jewellery, exotic food stuffs and other luxury items provided immense opportunities for enterprising merchants. Money-lending seems to have been confined to Hindus. Amir Hasan mentions that Muslim traders from Lahore travelled to Gujrat to do business with the Hindus, making huge profits in the bargain. Slave trade was a full-time or part-time business and was carried on by respectable people as well as the *ulema*.

Prosperity was shared by all nationalities and religious groups. Barani noted that in Delhi, Hindus lived like princes and maintained vast establishments. They employed "Mussalman servants to run in front of their mounts, even Muslims beg at their doors and within the city, the capital of the Muslim Sultanate, the infidels are addressed in such honourable terms as *rai, ranah, thakur, shaha, mehta* and *pundit*." He complains about, "the idolators and *mushriks* called *Kharji* and *zimmi* who are given rich dresses, horses and flags and are raised to high offices of State."[40]

According to the same author, "The Hindus and idol worshippers . . . had erected new temples in the city and environs." He quotes Sultan Firoz Shah as saying,"Every day the Hindus. . . pass below my palace beating cymbals and blowing conch-shells and perform idol-worship on the banks of the Jamna. While my name is being read in the Khutbah as the defender of Islam, these enemies of God and His Prophet, under my very eyes are proudly displaying their riches and live ostentatiously among the Muslims of my capital. They beat their drums and other musical instruments and perpetuate their pagan practices."[41]

However Barani's fanatacism embraced both Hindus and non-Sunni Muslims whom he condemned with equal fervour. "How can," he asks, "piety and righteousness be established when philosophers and heretics (*bad mazhaban*) who prefer Greek rationalism to the *Sunnah* and the *Shariah*, and who disbelieve the physical existence of heaven and hell are allowed to openly spread their doctrines? How can the religion of God triumph when these people, the enemies of God and His Prophet, live in the capital with dignity and ostentation and are not afraid to express their views?"[42]

The focal point of the city, like that of all medieval capitals, was of course, the court with the King as the Sun and the courtiers and hangers-on forming the constellations and offering warmth and comfort to the majority, and blistering heat to those on whom their wrath descended. In other words. Delhi was no different from the capital of any other great nation of the time. Here was a co-mingling of nationalities, creeds, languages and extremes of luxury and asceticism, all helping to form a colourful tapestry of beneficence and brutality, high thinking and low living, great learning and equally great ignorance, colour, rhythm, silence and clamour, grandeur and poverty, bravery and cowardice, orthodoxy and rationalism.

Delhi had become so magnificent and prosperous that many historians, out of reverence and respect called it Hazrat Delhi or simply The City.

Non-Muslim practices crept into the society even before the advent of the Turks in India. Muslims were already prostrating themselves before kings. The worship of the Sufi *Murshid* and his shrine arose out of reverence but owed a great deal to the Hindu reverence for anybody or anything showing signs of supernatural power. The mysticism of the Sufi and his strong bond with the common man welded a link in the chain that bound Hindus and Muslims together. The tombs of *Sheikh Muinuddin Chisti, Sheikh Nizamuddin Aulia, Sheikh Bakhtiyar Kaki* and a host of others in different parts of the country were visited by kings and commoners, Hindus and Muslims alike.[43]

Chewing of *pan* (no banquet could be rounded off without sereving pan) was one such practice. By the time of the Tughlaks, the offering of a '*bira*' to the bride had become an integral part of the marriage ceremony.

The caste system infiltrated Muslim society to the point of having different graveyards for Muslims of different professions. Dowry a concept alien to Islam, also became an integral part of the Muslim society and Firoz Tughlak provided dowry for Muslim orphan girls. Certain Indian phenomena, such as the monsoon, could only be expressed by the term *barshkal*. Muslims even of pure high born Turkish descent, adopted Indian names such as *Chajju, Kanchan, Hamidraja* etc. Converts from Hinduism, of course, maintained their ancestral practices but, with immigrants also adopting local customs it became impossible to differentiate between purely Hindu and Muslim customs.

The craft guilds continued in their age old way. Provisions for the court, nobility and army kept manufacturers of arms, saddles, tents, metal casting, weavers, stone cutters and a host of others fully employed. India's traditional trade also does not seem to have suffered because of the conquest.[44]

All this, of course; existed only in cities and towns where the majority of the Muslims dwelt. These were provided with all reasonable physical requirements and attributes of large flourishing urban centres with gardens, monuments, mosques, schools and bazaars providing all kinds of luxury and utilitarian articles.

The countryside continued as it had always done--the peasant tilling the land and the village industry providing basic needs. Although mostly concerned with urban affairs, the Sultans also attempted to keep the peasantry contented by providing water tanks, caravan serais and avoiding exorbitant taxation. "The peasant is the backbone of the State", Balban is reported to have said, "while he should not be allowed to develop into a rich potential rebel, ruinous exaction on him would cause a falling off in agriculture and the subsequent impoverishment of the State."[45]

Notes

1. Sir Syed Ahmad Khan, *Asar-us-sanadid*, pp. 7-23. Hereinafter referred to as Sir Syed.
2. R.E. Frykenberg ed., *Delhi through the Ages*. pp. xxxi-xxxvi. Hereinafter referred to as Frykenberg.
3. H.K. Kaul, *Historic Delhi: An Anthology*, 1985, pp. xxx-xxxii.
4. Sir Syed, pp. 12-13.
5. Archaeological Survey of India, *Four Reports Made during the Years 1862-63-64-65* by Alexander Cunningham, Simla, 1871, Vol.I, pp. 180-182
6. Mohamed Kasim Ferishta, *History of the Rise of the Muhammadan Power in India till the Year A.D. 1612*, p. 8.
7. C.F. Gorden Cumming, *In the Himalays and on the Indian Plains*, p. 220.
8. Thomas Seymour Burt, *Account of a Voyage in India*, Vol. 2, pp. 185-190.
9. W.H. Sleeman, *Rambles & Recollections of an Indian Official*, Vol. 2, pp. 253-55.
10. Jackson V, 'Delhi a vast Military Encampment', p. 19 in Frykenberg.
11. M. Habib, *Politics and Society during Early Medieval Period*, p. 83. Hereinafter referred to as Habib.
12. Minhaj-us-Siraj, *Tabaqat-i-Nasiri*, pp. 598-599. Hereinafter referred to as Minhaj.
13. R. Shamasastry, *Kautilya's Arthsastra*, pp. 51-55.
14. IbnBatuta, *Travels in Asia and Africa*, pp. 589-590. Hereinafter referred to as IbnBatuta.
15. Ibid., pp. 619-628.
16. Habib, p. 81.
17. Shihab-al-Din-al-Umri, *Masalik al absar fi-mamalik al Ansar. A fourteenth century Arab account of India under Sultan Mahammed bin Tughlaq*, pp. 35-36. Hereinafter referred to as Al-Umri.
18. Ibn Batuta, p. 624.
19. Al-Umri, p. 36.
20. M. Athar Ali, "Capital of the Sultans", p. 36, in Frykenberg.
21. A.B.M. Habibullah, *The Foundation of the Muslim Rule in India*, pp. 244-245. Hereinafter referred to as Habibullah.
22. Ibid. pp. 245-246.
23. Ibid. pp. 246-247.

24. Ibid. p. 247.
25. Ibid. p. 255.
26. Ibid. p. 254.
27. Habib, p. 82.
28. Al-Umri, p. 51.
29. Mohammad Wahib Mirza, *The Life and Works of Amir Khusrau*, p. 66.
30. Abdul Aziz Ameeq Hanfee, "The Historian in Khusrau", *Amir Khusrau Memorial Volume*. p. 180.
31. Shahab Sarmadee, *Life, Times and Works of Amir Khusrau Delavi*, pp. 245-247.
32. Minhaj, p. 387.
33. Zia-ud-din Barani, *Tarikh-i-Firoz-Shahi*, Elliot and Dowson, Vol. III, pp. 180-181. Hereinafter referred to as Barani.
34. M. Habib, p. 83.
35. Habibullah, p. 313.
36. Md. Habib, p. 81.
37. Ibn Batuta, pp. 737-738.
38. Al-Umri, p. 36.
39. Barani, p. 192.
40. K.A. Nizami, *Some Aspects of Religion and Politics in India during the Thirteenth Century*, p. 304.
41. Habibullah, pp. 253-56.
42. Ibid., p. 270.
43. Barani p. 217.
44. Quoted by Habibullah pp.273-74.
45. Habibullah, p. 259.

7

FATAWA -I -JAHANDARI

As quoted by Ibn-i-Hisham, Ibn-i-Khalduns Waquidi and others, the principles of the socio-political organisation of Islam were enunciated by the Prophet in his last speech at Mecca,thus:-'

> "Harken to my words, Oh men, for I know not whether
> I shall see you here another year".
> All customs of paganism have been abolished
> under my feet.
> The Arab is not superior to the non-Arab; the
> non-Arab is not superior to the Arab. You are all sons of Adam
> and Adam was made of the earth, Verily all
> Muslims are brothers.
> Your slaves! Feed them as you feed yourselves and
> dress them as you dress yourselves.
> The blood fueds of the Time of Ignorance are abolished.
> Remember Allah (in your dealings with) women. You have right over them and they have rights over you. Verily, you should consider each other's blood, property and reputation inviolable unto the Day of Judgement.
> Verily, a man is responsible for his own acts. A son is not responsible for the crimes of his father, nor is a father responsible for the crimes of his son. If a deformed Abyssinian slave holds authority over you and leads you according to the Book of Allah, obey him".[1]

This simple assertion of the equality of man, irrespective of his birth or position, the responsibility of each man for his actions and his right to the produce of his own labours, equality in dealings with women; and the obedience to a righteous leader underwent a complete transformation as the Arabs moved out of the confines of their homeland and established their rule in other countries. Such a simple creed could hardly be expected to hold its own in the face of the powerful Roman and Sassanid codes of law which held sway in large areas which the Arabs conquered, and which were, as it were, custom-tailored for imperial rule having been so crafted over centuries of experience.

These codes discriminated on grounds of birth, property, religion and sex in both criminal and civil cases and were designed to perpetuate such distinctions.

Gradually, Muslim polity took on these characteristics and, from being a simple religion of a rather primitive State, it took on the garb of imperialism, the king adopting all the trappings and panopoly of power that any imperial dynasty had ever used. This made it necessary to define political power, the rights and duties of kings,the general framework of the State and so on.

The *Fatawa-i-Jahandari* of Ziauddin Barani is a political thesis of the Sultanate period. It is an extremely interesting document because Barani liberally entwines his own prejudices with political theory to give the reader a rather clear concept of the character of the Delhi empire, which at that time could not, by any stretch of the imagination, have been classified as a theocratic State. Its basis was not *Shariat*, but *Zabita*, which "in the technique of administration", says Barani, "is a rule of action which a King imposes as an obligatory duty upon himself for realising the welfare of the State and from which he absolutely never deviates."[2]

Barani belonged to a noble family and was brought up to believe that aristocratic birth was the prime requisite for high office. He was frustrated and disillusioned because he was given no post by Alauddin Khalji, although he was a courtier of Muhammad bin Tughlak for 27 years. Under Firoz Shah, charges were levied against him and, in his 70th year, he was interned at Bhatner. He describes himself as white haired, old, bent, half-blind, friendless and unable to borrow any money. In spite of these handicaps, he wrote the two great books of the Sultanate period, "*Tarikh-i-Firoz Shahi*" and the "*Fatawa-i-Jahandari*", the latter being an attempt to put into coherent form, the political philosophy, the basic ideas of which he had already expressed in the earlier work.

The *Fatawa* is written in the form of an exhortation by Sultan Mahmud of Ghazni to his sons and other Sultans. Apart from Mahmud, a contemporary of the Sultan and Barani himself are made to speak.

Barani had no real knowledge of the Sultan but probably used him to give authority to his own philosophy which he aired through the monarch's utterances to escape criticism.

Although Barani quotes Utbi, Baihaqi, Minhaj etc, he seems to have had no first hand knowledge of their works, or if he did, he had forgotten it all, probably because of his age, by the time he came to write this book.

Barani's emphasis on the superiority of the upper classes, which forms the basic feature of the *Fatawa*, is sometimes carried to rather ridiculous extremes. He asserts that since low-class Muslims could, with proper education, reach high positions and oust the high born incumbents from them, the State had a duty to prevent them from achieving such education.

Even piety becomes the privilege of the high born. According to the author, any person showing marked piety, even though he be low born, must have aristocratic blood in his veins. He condemns conversion since Islam, according to him, can come to a man only through heredity. To be spiritually effective, a man must be born a Muslim.[3]

Barani asserts the low born are "not to be taught reading and writing for plenty of disorders arise owing to the skill of the low born in knowledge".[4]

Further he says, "Even if a man of base or low birth is adorned with a hundred merits he will not be able to organise and administer the country according to expectations or be worthy of leadership and political trust."[5]

"The merits and demerits of men have been apportioned at the beginning of time and allotted to their souls. . . . So all the arts, fine and coarse, from writing and horsemanship to hair cutting and tanning--in accordance with the merits and demerits which by their basic nature had been allotted to their soul-- were communicated to the minds and breasts of men. . . . This aptitude for arts, fine and coarse, is hereditary.... And as excellences have been put into those who have adopted the nobler professions, they alone are capable of virtues. . . . These groups alone are worthy of offices and posts in the government of the King."[6]

Such lines as the above could easily have been penned by a caste conscious. Hindu, so great is the emphasis on birth and pre--destination. In fact, they are a good index to the extent of Hindusation to which even the bigoted Muslim intellectuals had fallen prey in a little over a century of the establishment of Muslim rule in India.

But this was, perhaps, the ultimate protest against the political power of the low-born, the Chihalgani, the Forty Slaves, who controlled the empire of Delhi after the death of Iltutmish and to the men of humble birth whom Muhammad bin Tughlak appointed to high position because of their loyalty and efficiency.

However, Barani was a devout Muslim and he enumerates among the duties of a good King "... to ensure the greatness of the True word, the supremacy of the Muslim religion, the suppression and overthrow of the opponents and enemies of the Faith, the execution of the orders of religion and the maintenance of their own authority." To this end, he advocates the adoption by Muslim kings of non-Islamic customs such as those followed by Iranian emperors "So that they may utilise their authority and strength for the protection and promotion of the Faith, for ensuring the greatness of the True word by constant holy wars intended to overthrow idolatory and polytheism and for raising the prestige of Islam by killing and slaughtering the enemies of the Faith." "Nevertheless", says Barani, "Islam totally forbids and prohibits the inequities committed by the Iranian emperors." "But," he continues, "just as the eating of carrion is yet permitted in times of dire need, similarly the customs and traditions of the pagan emperors of Iran ... should, from the viewpoint of truth and correct Faith, be considered like the eating of a carrion in time of dire need".[7]

The book deals with, among others, the powers and duties of a king, the benefits of consultation and good advice; qualities of important officials, the administration of justice, quality and quantity of punishment etc. There is loud protestation of the uniqueness and total sanctity of Islamic laws and a cheerful permission to circumvent them in a variety of ways with the exhortation "You should give plenty of charities in compensation and be afraid of your sins."

Pragmatically he asserts, "If there is anything in these laws (made by the king) against the Sunnah and you find their enforcement to be nevertheless necessary owing to the lack of virtue or the extreme weakness of faith among the people ...... It should be clear to you that the enforcement of these laws comes under the category of the Shariat precept:

"Necessities make lawful things forbidden."[8]

There is a clear distinction drawn between the private and public life of a king. Barani states categorically "The policy of the state is distinct from the personal life of the king; it would, of course, be appropriate for kings to set the example of obeying the laws they impose on others, but the fact that they are themselves falling into sinfulness is irrelevant to the functioning of their governments.[9]

"The test of the king 's faith is that he keeps the inhabitants of his kingdom on the path of righteous law (Shariat) Even if he is involved in personal sins, owing to his (Physical) desire, yet through the dignity and power of his kingship he maintains the authority of the Shariat in such a way and so firmly enforced are all his commands and prohibitions that no one can openly practice anything against the law in his country".[10]

"Prophethood," declares Barani, "is the perfection of religion and kingship is the perfection of worldly good fortune" thus placing secular and religious authorities firmly on the same basis.[11]

Kingship is defined simply as " the control which a man obtains over a territory by power or force. He may also be entitled to it (by inheritance) and may be thus maintaining what is his own or he may have obtained it by usurpation and without any right. In either case, they call him king on account of his control of the territory."[12]

No king should be guided by his own desires or instinct. Wise counsellors are necessary for good government and their advice must be heard. They must be acquainted with the secrets of the State; they should have perfect security for their lives and posts so that they have no compulsion to resort to flattery or be afraid to speak their minds.

They should be men of equal knowledge, intelligence and loyalty and be allowed to express their opinions before the king speaks, so that their opinion would not be influenced by his convictions. "All errors into which kings have fallen have been due to the fact that their decisions have been in consonance with their passions and have, therefore, appeared to them to be good and pleasing. But as the decisions which they considered to be good were really erroneous, they had failed to discern the merits and demerits of their counsellors and ended by throwing their kingdoms to the winds by following injudicious and wrong decisions."

"The first condition of consultation is the frank expression of opinions by the counsellors that is, in the Royal Consultative Council (*Majlis-i-Rai*). All counsellors should be able to say, whatever comes to their mind about the execution of State enterprises, to give reasons and arguments for their opinions and to discuss frankly with each other."[13]

The choice of his advisers and officials, marks a king as a sagacious and able ruler. All wise men of ancient and modern times are agreed on this fact--that the merits or vices of the supporters, helpers, high officers and partisans of the king are a conclusive proof of the merits or vices (as the case may be) of the king himself.[14] "There is not, and cannot be, a greater source of pride and glory for a king than a wise wazir, who is inspired with correct judgement. Without a wise wazir kingship is in vain...."[15]

Justice

"Justice", says Barani, "is the balance in which the actions of the people, good or bad, are weighed. The distinction between righteous and wrongful claims is clarified by justice."[16]

"Through their royal power and prestige, the kings can prevent the strong from having recourse to oppression in their dealings with the poor."

"No religion which is founded on Divine Commandment (Ahkam) can do without justice." "The real justification for the supremacy of kings and of their power and dignity is the need for enforcing justice."[17]

Barani, along with other matters, also deals with price control. According to him "They (kings) should understand that the stability of their kingdom depends upon the stability of the army and the people, and that the stability of the army and the people depends upon the low price of the means of livelihood."[18]

While Barani demanded strong punishment for religious offences he protested strongly against vendettas directed against the women and children of political offenders. Since the *Shariat* was silent on the question of political punishments, Barani himself sought to discover some principles for regulating them on the basis of secular reason and humanity.[19]

Notes

1. K.A. Nizami, *Some Aspects of Religion and Politics in India during the Thirteenth Century*, p. 3.
2. M. Habib & Afsar Umar Salim Khan, *The Political Theory of the Delhi Sultanate*, including a translation of Zia-ud-Din Barani's *Fatawa-i-Jahandari*, p. 64.
3. Ibid., pp. i, ii, iii.
4. Ibid., p. 49.
5. Ibid., p. 95.
6. Ibid., pp. 97-98.
7. Ibid., pp. 39-40.
8. Ibid., p. 65.
9. Ibid., p. 3.
10. Ibid., p. 3.

11. Ibid., p. 35.
12. Ibid., p. 95.
13. Ibid., p. 11.
14. Ibid., p. 96.
15. Ibid., p. 93.
16. Ibid., p. 10.
17. Ibid., p. 16.
18. Ibid., p. 35.
19. Ibid., p. xi.

8

RELIGION AND POLITICS

Arabs had been trading with India from pre-historic times, bringing such commodities as horses and Persian Gulf pearls and taking away, among others, Indian sugar textiles and swords. This commerce continued even after the rise of Islam and the conversion of all Arabs to the Muslim faith. On the Malabar coast of South India, Arabs were treated as special guests, were called Moplah, meaning guest or son-in-law, and were allotted plots of land in the suburbs of cities for residential purposes and thus were able to rise to high positions in the Government.[1]

The conquest of Sind by Muhammad bin Qasim brought an added dimension to the relationship. Sind broke away from the Caliphate and became an independent Indian kingdom under the Ismailis or Carmathians, a sect regarded as heretics by the orthodox Sunnis who formed the ruling class in Baghdad and most Islamic kingdoms.

Muslim settlements had grown up in various places in North India and Muslim merchants continued the trade started by their pre-Islamic forefathers.[2]

Living among a sea of Hindus, the Muslims maintained their culture. Shaikh Bahauddin Zakariya, whose ancestors had been living in India for three generations, was born in Kangra in 1192 AD and was so well-versed in the Arabic language that when he went to Arabic speaking Muslim countries for further studies he had no language difficulty. Though the Muslim community at Kannauj disappeared, the one at Badaun continued to flourish and the city became a great centre of Muslim learning and culture.Maulana Raziuddin Hasan Sanghani (1181-1252AD) studied the Prophet's traditions (*Hadia*) at Badaun so thoroughly, that when he went to Baghdad he was immediately recognised as a great scholar. His "*Mashariqual Anwar*", a collection of *hadises*, is considred to be one of the most reliable.[3]

Sanskrit works such as *Brahmsiddhanta* of Brahmagupta and his *Khanda Khandyaka* had already been translated into Arabic and the Arabs carried the Indian knowledge of astronomy and numerals and Indian philosophy to Europe. After the Arab conquest of Sind, they took Indian masons and painters to build and embellish mosques and palaces.[4]

The two communities, thus, were familiar with each other's manners, customs, religious rites and so on. They also traded commodities and skills to mutual benefit. For instance, Mohammad bin Qasim had the monopoly of the *munjaniq* (catapult) which facilitated his conquest of Sind, but by the 12th century, every Indian fort was plentifully supplied with *munjaniqs* and a Muslim contingent formed part of most Hindu armies.

It is obvious that the successful inroads of Mahmud of Ghazni depended strongly on knowledge of local terrain, trades routes and resources which were probably obtained from Muslim merchants.[5]

The violence of his incursions created justifiable anti-Muslim feelings among Hindus.He looted, pillaged and killed as he went along and his actions led to the conclusion that it was the result of communal frenzy - that Mahmud's activities in India were that of a fervent Muslim trying to destroy heathens as enjoined by Islam. Nothing could be further from the truth. If we study the history of the Middle East, we find Muslims fighting and destroying each other with equal frenzy, while in India the Hindu Thakur or Rajput put his co-religionist adversary to the sword with an equal amount of gusto.

When Mahmud's son-in-law Abul Abbas-i-Maimun Farighuni was murdered by some of his troops, Mahmud went in person to avenge his death. He defeated the insurgents, put the ringleader and murderers to the sword and reduced the territory under his sway.[6]

As the Turkish salves in India owed loyalty only to their master, having no family or homeland to detract from their allegiance, so too the Indian salves (obviously Hindu) in Ghazni were totally loyal to the ruler and were considered absolutely dependable. They had their own commander, the *Sipahsalar-i-Hinduyan* and their own quarters in the city,They formed an important part of the infantry and were considered to be good fighters, their religion being no hindrance to their being employed to fight Muslim or Christian enemies.[7] After the suppression of the revolt in Sistan in 1000 AD Mahmud's Hindu soldiers behaved with extreme savagery, sacking the Friday mosque of Zarang and massacring the Muslims in it, besides killing the Christians in the churches.[8]

Mahmud's son appointed a Hindu, Tilak, as his Viceroy in Lahore. In Ramazan 425 AH (July 1033), notes Baihaqi, "news came that Ahmad Nialtigin had captured Lahore"...but it was reported that Tilak Hindu had collected a powerful army from every detachment and quarter and was advancing in that direction; that the heart of that vile rebel was quaking within him and that there was a space of only two *kos* between the two armies. The *Amir* read this despatch while he was drinking and ordered a letter to Tilak Hindu to be written and placed in its case. He directed Tilak to proceed against Ahmad with all speed. The Amir sealed the letter and added a postscript with his own hand, written with all force which characterised his style, imperious and at the same time appropriate to the person addressed. This was concealed from his confidential *Diwan* and sent off with all haste."[9]

He continues, "In Zi-kada 425 (September & October 1034) the Sultan received intelligence that when Tilak arrived at Lahore he took several Muslim friends of Ahmad prisoner and ordered their right hands to be cut off... that Tilak, in full confidence and power, pursued Ahmad with a large body of men, chiefly Hindus; that in the pursuit several skirmishes and actions took place... that a severe engagment ensued when Ahmad, who not able to stand his ground, was defeated and took to flight."[10]

Tilak wrote letters to the Hindu Jats, who were helping Nialtigin "to desert the cause of that godless man and to remember that whoever should bring him or his head should receive a reward of 500,000 dirhams." The Jats, obeying Tilak, killed Ahmad and when they demanded the reward Tilak bargained with them and persuaded them to accept a sum of 100,000 *dirhams*.

The *Amir* ordered congratulatory letters to be written expressing his obligation to Tilak and the others and praised them for their conduct.[11]

The attitude on both sides of the border, in Ghazni as well as in India, seems to have been the same. It was the imperative of the situation rather than the religion of the adversary or subordinate that dictated the course of action or pledging of loyalty. As Mahmud did not hesitate to set Kafirs to massacre the "people of the Book", so the Jats did not hesitate to ally themselves against their co-religionist Tilak.

One more example of co-religionist barbarity would serve to illustrate the point. The family of Ghur bitterly hated Mahmud and his descendents for having conquered Ghazni which they claimed as their property. Ala-ud-din, uncle of Muhammad bin Sam of Ghur took back Ghazani, says Minhaj, " by storm, and during seven nights and seven days, fired the place and burnt it with obstinacy and wantonness". He continues, "The chronicler states that, during these seven days, the air, from the blackness of the smoke, continued as black as night, and those nights, from the flames raging in the burning city, were lighted up as light as day. During these seven days, likewise, rapine, plunder and massacre were carried on with the utmost pertinacity and vindictiveness. All the men that were found were killed and the women and children were made captive."[12]

After this, he ravaged other cities belonging to Mahmud's dynasty, killed high officers and even went to the extent of exhuming the remains of certain Sultans from their graves and having them burnt.[13]

According to the Middle Eastern concept, whether Mongol or Turk, apparently power had to be ruthlessly wielded for it to be appreciated and obeyed.

Mahmud's incursions into India were mostly in search of plunder. He came for the untold wealth that was in the country, a large portion of which happened to be found in the great Indian temples. When he came to Mathura, for instance, he found nearly a thousand palaces of stone and a temple of such size and grandeur that "if a thousand times a thousand dinars should be expended and builders and workmen of the greatest activity and energy should be employed for two hundred years, they could not complete the like." Within this building were five idols of gold, five *gaz* or ells in height, and the eyes of one of them were formed of two rubies which were valued at 50,000 dinars of gold. The eyes of another were formed of two saphires, of the weight of four hundred *miskals* (600= 1 ser= 1 lb 13 ozs.) the immense value of which could not be computed. From the lower extremities of one of the idols, pure gold of the weight of 4400 *miskals* was obtained. Besides these great idols, there were two hundred others of silver, in the temple, the whole of which were broken up and the temple itself was overthrown.[14]

In the famed magnificent temple of Somnath, the treasure captured exceeded 20 lakh *dinars*.[15]

The enormous wealth of the temples had tempted Hindus also to plunder them. A large number of Jain temples at Dabhoi and Cambay near Anhilwara in Gujarat were plundered by the Paramara King, Subhatavarman, of Malwa between 1193 and 1210 AD. King Harsha of the 2nd Lohara dynasty of Kashmir plundered a number of Hindu temples for replenishing his treasury.[16]

Mosques were never looted for they were starkly simple structures and offered no temptation to any one. Ornamentation was usually restricted to elaborate tile work or carving in marble or wood. Occasionally, some gold or silver would be used but never enough to make them a target of greed. They offered education and sanctuary in items of need but were never repositories of treasure.

The Indian forts also yielded immense wealth. After the capture of the fort of Nagarkot, near Kangra, Utbi, Mahmud's historian, records "the treasures were laden on the backs of as many camels as they could procure and the officers carried away the rest. The stamped coin amounted to 70,000 royal dirhams and the gold and silver ingots amounted to 7 lakhs and 400 mans in weight besides wearing apparel and fine cloths of Sus, respecting which old men said that they never remembered to have seen so fine, soft and embroidered a cloth. Among the booty was a house of white silver, like the houses of rich men, the length of which was thirty yards and the breadth fifteen. It could be taken to pieces and put together again. And there was a canopy made of the linen of Rum 40 yards long and 20 broad, supported on two gold and two silver poles which had been cast in moulds." [17]

Alberuni

The only account of India at the time of Mahmud's invasion has been given by Abu Raihan Muhammad Ibn Ahmad Alberuni. Born in Khwarizm, now called Khiva[18] Alberuni was brought by Mahmud to Ghazni in accordance with his passion for bringing back from his conquests huge libraries and learned men to his court. Baihaqi reports, that when he came across a man or woman who was an expert in any skill, he deported them thither (to Ghazna). Since every medieval king prided himself on his patronage of the arts, Mahmud too filled his capital with luminaries in all fields of art and literature. He and his sons were well versed in Arabic and Persian classics and Islamic theology. There were 400 poets in regular attendance on Mahmud, presided over by the Amir-Ash-Shuara (Poet laureate) who was kept busy commemorating his master's exploits in verse.

Alberuni writes that honouring learning and its representatives "is... the duty of those who rule over them, of kings and princes. For they alone can free the minds of scholars from the daily anixeties for the necessities of life and stimulate their energies to earn more fame and favour. The yearning for which is the pith and marrow of human nature."[19]

Alberuni was a noted scholar who was obviously well acquainted with Hindu writing and philosophy. He has quoted among others, works like the *Samkhya by* Kaoila; *Book of Patanjali*; *Gita*; *Vishnu Purana*; *Manusmriti*; *Caraka Samhita* and the commentary of the *Khandakhadyaka* by Balabhadra. He was also well versed in Greek, Christian and Jewish theologies. In order to make Hindu ideas understandable to his Muslim readers, he illustrated them with the ones they were acquainted with.[20] He seems also to be have had knowledge of Indian works on snakes, poison, auguring, ethics and politics, veterinary art and science of war. He studied the Arabic translations but, when necessary, went back to the original Sanskrit sources, making new and more accurate translations and testing the date of Indian astronomers by calculation.[21]

He seemed to have travelled freely about a large part of India talking to people and studying their customs and ideas.

Says Sachau "Judging Alberuni in relation to his predecessors we come to the conculsion that his work formed a most marked progress. His description of Hindu philosophy was probably unparalleled. His system of chronology and astronomy was more complete and accurate than had ever before been given. His communications from the Puranas were probably entirely new to his readers as also important chapters on literature, manners, festivals, actual geography and the much quoted chapter on historic chronology."[22]

It is this objectivity which gives credence and value to his work. He desists from comments on matters that seem incongruous to him, writing "to such things silence is the only proper answer". He manages to convince the reader of his genuine desire to understand even the most strange things, so that when he finds in the works of Varahamihira, along with good scientific work, parts that appear to him like "the ravings of a madman" one knows that he is expressing his frustration rather than talking down at an inferior people.It is this objectivity, perhaps, that makes him quote extensively from both classical authors and living persons allowing the Hindus' own idea and views to come to the reader in a more or less undiluted form.[23]

Hieun Tsang

Alberuni's account is the first foreigner's account of conditions in India after that of the Chinese pilgrim Hieun T'Sang who was in India from 629 to 643 A.D. The Chinese had recorded two great assemblies, one at Kannauj and the other at Prayag attended by 20 kings and thousands of Buddhist, Jain and Brahmin theologians and priests. Images of the Buddha, Adityadeva (The Sun) and Isvaradeva (Siva) were installed on successive days.[24]

Indians maintained relations with their neighbours and with countries as far away as Rome. The overland route to China was much travelled. Sir Aurel Stein who excavated the ruins of Buddhist monastries and stupas, and found Buddhist & Brahmanical idols and manuscripts in Central Asia, remarked that he could have believed himself to be in the familier surroundings of an ancient Indian city in the Punjab.[25]

Maritime adventure also found votaries. The eastern coast of India was studded with ports from which Indians sailed forth to establish trading relations with South East Asia and later to conquer lands and establish kingdoms. Between the 2nd and 5th centuries AD parts of the Malaya Peninsula, Cambodia, Annam, Sumatra, Java, Bali and Borneo were all colonised. Brahamanism flourished here along with Buddhism. Naturally, language, alphabet, social manners and customs were all Indian in origin. Some of these kingdoms outlasted Hindu rule in India.[26]

By the time Alberuni reached India in the 11th century, the picture had completely changed. Brahmanism held total sway and Indians had enclosed themselves firmly within their frontiers and become highly suspicious of everything foreign. The crossing of the sea was declared a sin,[27] and a spirit of rather pompous self satisfaction pervaded the land. The stratification of caste had become so rigid that it rent the fabric of society and made it unable to face any serious challenge.

Alberuni must have been quite staggered at the strength of the caste system and the barriers it set up, but he reports the fact in a matter of fact way, "I have repeatedly been told that when Hindu slaves (in Muslim countries) escape and return to their country and religion, the Hindus order that they should fast by way of expiation, then they bury them in the dung, and milk of cows for a certain number of days till they get into a state of fermentation. Then they drag them out of the dirt and give them similar dirt to eat and more of the like.

"I have asked the Brahmans if this is true, but they deny it and maintain that there is no expiation possible for such an individual, and that he is never allowed to return into those conditions of life in which he was before he was carried off as a prisoner. And how should that be possible? If a Brahman eats in the house of a sudra for sundry days he is expelled from his caste and can never regain it." [28]

About the inward looking qualities of the Hindus he writes, "... the Hindus believe there is no country but theirs; no nation like theirs, no kings like theirs, no religion like theirs, no science like theirs. They are haughty, foolishly vain, self-conceited and stolid. They are by nature niggardly in communicating that which they know and they take the greatest possible care to withhold it from men of another caste among their own people, still much more, of course, from any foreigners.... Their haughtiness is such that if you tell them of any science or scholar in Khorasan and Persia they will think you to be an ignoramus and a liar. If they travelled and mixed with other nations they would soon change their mind for their ancestors were not as narrow minded as the present generation." He says that when he discussed scientific matters with them and pointed out the rules of logical deduction and the scientific basis of all mathematics he was asked which Hindu master had taught him all he knew.[29]

While not mincing words about what he considered the shortcomings of the Hindus, Alberuni considered them excellent philosophers, mathematicians and astronomers as well as good builders. About the construction of ponds in Hindu holy places he says, "In this they have attained a high degree of art, so that our people, when they see them, wonder at them and are unable to describe them, much less to construct anything like them.[30]

Road Network

Alberuni travelled over large parts of the country which were obviously connected by excellent roads. Taking Kannauj in U.P. as the central point, the writer mentions various roads going in different directions--to Kashmir, Ghazna and Kabul passing through Panipat, Jhelum and Jalandhar. Somnath, Anhilwara (Patan) and *Bayana* were all connected by road to Kannauj. The last was also connected to Malwa from where 2 main roads went to Mandakir (Malkhet) on the Godavari and the other to Thana (Bombay). Other places connected to the city were Multan in Punjab from where a road went to Loharani in Sind (near Karachi). Still another road connected it with Broach.

There were roads going off to Sylhet and Bihat (in Kamarupa) and to Gangasair (mouth of the Ganges) passing through Ajudhya, Benaras, Patliputra and Dukampur.

A highway connected Tanut near Bihat in the north-east, with a point just about 3 miles from Tibet passing through Nepal and Bhuteshar.

From the latter,a highway going northwest across Tibet reached Kashmir.

The South is also mentioned with names like Rameshare (Rameshwaram) which is said to be opposite Sarandib and Sethubandha (Bridge of the Ocean), said to have been built by Rama to the castle of Lanka, is placed at two *farsakh* from Rameshar.[31]

Prayaga and Somnath

Alberuni describes some sacred places of the Hindus, among them Prayaga and Somnath. "At the junction of the two rivers, Yamuna and Ganga, there is a great tree called Prayaga,a tree of the species called *vata*. It is peculiar to this kind of tree that its branches send forth two species of twigs, some directed upward, as is the case with all trees, and others directed downward like roots, but without leaves. If such a twig enters into the soil, it is like a supporting column to the branch whence it has grown. Nature has arranged this on purpose, since the branches of this tree are of an enormous extent and require to be supported. Here the Brahmans and Kshatriyas are in the habit of committing suicide by climbing up the tree and throwing themselves into the Ganga."[32]

Relating the story of the great temple of Somnath, Alberuni says that it was a linga erected by the Moon as penance for favouritism towards one of his wives against the others--all the wives were the daughters of Prajapati who, hearing their complaint, admonished the Moon to correct his behaviour.When the latter took no notice, Prajapati cursed him and his face became leprous. Somnath means master of the moon. Each time the moon rose and set, the water of the ocean on the banks of which Somnath stood, rose high to cover the place where the temple stood. When the moon reached the meridian of noon and midnight, the water receded in the ebb and the place again became visible. The moon, thus, was perpetually occupied in bathing the idol and serving it.

According to Alberuni a jug of Ganges water and flowers from Kashmir were brought to Somnath everyday.The idol was believed to have the power to cure people of chronic and incurable diseases. He says that Somnath became famous because it was a harbour for seafaring people and a station for those who travelled between Sufalats in the country of the žanj and China. He put the age of the temple at the time of its destruction at 100 years.

While being critical of the Hindus, Alberuni is also outspoken against the early Muslims who destroyed the great civilisation of Iran, and compares the Arabs with Zoroastrians to the detriment of the former.[33]

Showing courage of a high order, in those days of fawning courtiers and flattering historians, Alberuni criticises Mahmud's actions without mincing any words. "Mahmud", he writies, "ruined the prosperity of the country and performed there wonderful exploits by which the Hindus became like atoms scattered in all directions and like a tale of old in the mouths of the people. Their scattered remains cherish, of course, the most inveterate aversion towards all Muslims. This is the reason, too, why Hindu scientists have retired away from those parts of the country conquered by us and have fled to places which our hand cannot yet reach, to Kashmir, Benaras and other places. And there the antagonism between them and all foreigners receives more and more nourishment both from political and religious sources."[2]

Caste

Hindus lived in fortified cities, towns and villages but only the higher castes lived within the walls. Sudras and *Vaisyas* were allowed to enter the fortifications at fixed times to render services and to supply commodities. At night they were sent out into their houses in the countryside where they were exposed to all sorts of dangers. Much earlier the Manusmriti had prescribed, "The dwellings of the Chandolas and the Schwapachas shall be outside the village, they shall be made Apapatras, and their wealth shall be dogs and donkeys. Their dress (shall be) garments of the dead; (they shall) eat their food from broken dishes, black iron (shall be) their ornament and they shall always wander from place to place. A man who fulfils a religious duty shall not seek intercourse with them, their transactions (shall be) among themselves, and their marriages with their equals. Their food shall be given to them by others (than an Aryan giver) in a broken dish; at night they shall not walk about in villages and in towns. By day they may go about for purposes of their work, distinguished by marks of the King's command, and they shall carry out the corpses (of persons) who have no relations; that is a settled rule. Dying without the expectation of a reward, for the sake of Brahmans and, of course, or in the defence of women and childern, secures beatitude to those excluded (from the Aryan community).[35]

"A chandala, a village pig, a cock, a dog, a menstruating woman and an eunuch must not look at the Brahmans while they eat."[36]

Sudras and *Vaisyas* were allowed to meditate on God although "Every action", says Alberuni, "which is the privilege of a Brahman such as saying prayers, recitation of the Vedas and offering sacrifices to fire, is forbidden to him to such a degree that when, for example, a Sudra or a Vaisya is proved to have recited the Veda, he is accused by the Brahmans before the ruler and the latter will order his tongue to be cut off."[37]

Of the Brahman the Manusmriti says, "He is, by right, the lord of this whole creation. A Brahman coming into existence, is born as the highest on earth, the lord of all created beings, for the protection of the treasury of the law. Whatever exists in the world is the property of the Brahman, on account of the excellence of his origin the Brahman is, indeed, entitled to it all. He alone deserves to possess this whole earth." A Sudra, though emancipated by his master, is not released from servitude; since that is innate in him, who can set him free?"[38]

The Brahmans, secure in their role as the world's elite played no real political role. Their only loyalty was to their own group and not even to the ruler. In fact, they were responsible for the fall of the Sena dynasty in the 13th century, by prophesying its downfall and spreading panic.

Rae Lakhmaniah, the ruler of Nudiah, who according to Minhaj, "was a very great Rae" was told by astrologers and other wise men of his kingdom that according to their books the Turks, having conquered Bihar, would soon reach his kingdom. When the Rae asked for specific identification marks of the man destined to conquer his territory he was told that "...when he stands upright on his two feet and lets down his two hands, his hands will reach beyond the point of his knees in such wise that the fingers will touch the calves of his legs." The Rae sent trusted men to investigate the matter and they reported that the physical characteristics of Muhammad-i-Bakhtiyar-i-Khalji corresponded to this description.

Most of the inhabitants including, of course, the Brahmans left the city but the Rae stayed on. When Bakhtiyar-i-Khalji reached the fortress of Bihar with a small band of men, the ruler Rae Lakhmaniah was "seated at the head of his table, and dishes of gold and silver, full of victuals, were placed according to his accustomed routine when a cry arose from the gateway of the Rae's palace and the interior of the city. By the time he became certain what was the state of affairs, Muhammad-i-Bakhtiyar had dashed forwards through the gateway into the palace, and had put several persons to the sword. The Ree fled barefooted by the back part of the palace; and the whole of his treasures, his wives and (other) females, his domestic servants, his particular attendants, were taken, and the Mussalmans captured a number of elephants and such a vast amount of booty fell to their lot, as cannot be recorded.''[39]

Method of Fighting

The Hindu army was large but the privilege of fighting belonged only to a high born warrior caste. The Thakurs fought in the same way as the knights of Europe, a small elitist class whose number could never be increased. The fighting was done to fixed rules and there seems to have been no attempt to study the strategy of the enemy or to try to circumvent his tactics. Therefore any deviation from the fixed norms of warfare practiced by the Thakurs could throw them into disarray and secure cheap victory for the assailant. The Thakurs or Rajputs, were personally very brave and great swordsmen who regarded each battle as a ''tournament in which to display their skill, bravery and chivalry. Babar noted in his diary in 1526 that Indians knew how to die but not how to fight. They lacked the capacity of taking advantage of the enemy's weakness and making of feints and manoeuvres on the battlefield.''[1]

It is a remarkable fact that even though great treatises have been written on war and strategy, no real attempt have ever been made in India to study the techniques of war followed by the enemy. The Rajput code of chivalry dictated that no defeated man should come home alive. Every one perished on the battlerfield whether by the enemy's or his own sword. This wanton waste of the flower of the country's best fighting men was never taken into account. The value of withdrawal and remassing in order to assess the situation and come up with better solutions was never considered. In fact, it was considered despicable and the coward's way out-something to be avoided at all costs.

Muhammad bin Sam of Ghur was defeated by the Rai of Gujrat in 1178 and by Rai Pithora at Tarain in 1191. It was thus not his great soldierly qualities but strategy that made him ruler of Delhi. His victory in 1192 was due merely to the fact that he attacked early in the morning--a move for which the Rais trained in rigid patterns of warfare were totally unprepared.

Historians have found it difficult to explain the rapid advance of the Muslim power in India . Within a short space of 13 years the invaders had conquered the whole area of North India stretching from Punjab to parts of Assam.Various explanations such as superior cavalry and arms have been given as reasons for this success. However, Arabic horses and the catapult had been available to Indians long before the Turkish invasion and India produced formidable weapons.[41]

The Faulad-i-Hind, the Indian sword, with an amazing cutting edge, caught Mahmud's eye and he enquired about the secret of its excellence. To the iron block, he was told,was added an ingot of silver. This was heated and the sword was shaped. The edge was then sharpened by being smeared with a paste and then turning against a wheel.[42]

Elephants had been used in India for ages and were an indication of the power and prestige of Indians. They had earlier been used in the Middle East by the Sasanids in Persia but for purely ceremonial purposes.Their use in war was first attempted by the Ghazni Sultans whose elephants came as booty of war and tribute from Indian princes. Mahmud captured 350 elephants from Kannauj and 185 from Mahaban in 1018-19. Utbi records that Mahmud's expedition to Thanesar in 1014 was provoked by his desire to acquire some elephants especially bred for war. On another occasion, the Sultan so coveted an elephant that he offered 50 ordinary ones in exchange.[43]

It was, therefore, neither better manpower nor superior arms that were responsible for the virtual rout of Hindu power but better strategy. The Sultans almost every time, had the survey of a prospective battlefield made and took the typography into account before engaging in battle, which enabled them to cut off food supplies and divert water channels to deprive their opponents of food and water. As against the Rajputs's traditional three divisions-- rights, left and centre -- the invaders had five , the two additional ones being the advance Guard and the Reserve. Also Indians fought mainly with swords while the Turks favoured archery which gave them the advantage of attacking from a distance.[44]

The Indian elephants were frightened to such an extent by the Turkish cavalry manoeuvres that they turned and fled trampling Indian soldiers to death.

Battle of Tarain

Minhaj-us-Siraj describes the battle of Tarain where Muhammad Ghuri defeated Rai Pithora. ''The centre division of the army, the baggage, the standards and banners, his canopy of state and the elephants, were left several miles in the rear. He marshalled his ranks and was advancing leisurely. The light armed and unencumbered horsemen, he had directed should be divided into four divisions and had appointed them to act against the infidels on four sides; and the Sultan had commanded saying: "It is necessary that, on the right and left, and front and rear, 10,000 mounted archers should keep the infidel host in play; and when their elephants, horsemen and foot advance to the attack, you are to face about and keep the distance of a horse's course in front of them." "The Mussalman troops acted according to these instructions and having exhausted and wearied the unbelievers, Almighty God gave the victory to Islam and the infidel host was overthrown.[45]

The Rajput troops were attacked by the reserve troops at the end of the day when the former were exhausted.[46]

Srivastava has summed up the Hindu situation in two pithy sentences. "Mere physical strength and military weapons do not constitute the total equipment of an army," "an inspiring ideology is as essential as military training and equipment."[47]

Srivastava further links the Indian failure with the rigidity of the caste structure. He writies, " The Jats, Meds and certain other castes were looked down upon by the ruler, the court and the official class no less than by the higher caste people. They were not allowed to ride on saddled horses, to carry arms or to put on fine clothes. Owing to these circumstances, social solidarity, the best guarantee of political independence, was consipicuously lacking--there was little sympathy between the people and their king ... owing to these causes many of Dahir's (Ruler of Sind) subjects, particularly the Buddhists and the traders, refused to fight on the plea that it was none of their business. Quite a number of them supplied valuable information to the invader and joined him against their king and country."[49]

He continues, "As far as India was concerned it learnt no lesson and our people. . . were found as unprepared and as indifferent to the happenings outside three centuries later, when the Turks bagan hammering the gate of their frontiers, as in the early years of the 8th century when Muhammad bin Qasim took Dahir by surprise."[45]

Rajputs

Somewhere between the invasions of the Ghaznavid Sultan (999-1030) and the establishment of Turkish rule in India (1191-92) the Rajputs came into power. They are never mentioned by Alberuni according to whom rulers were styled Thakurs, Rawats and so on. However, in the 12th century the political scene was dominated by the Chauhans of Sambhar and Ajmer, the Paramaras of Malwa, the Kalachuris of Chedi, the Chandelas of Bundelkhand, the Chalukyas of Gujrat, the Gahadavals of Kannauj, the Palas of Magadha, the Suras and, later, the Senas of Bengal.[50]

The rulers belonged to the Kshatriya or warrior caste whose caste duty was fighting as a result of which warfare was a constant feature between independent kingdoms. This made for fluctuating frontiers and fortunes. Each kingdom was divided into fiefs held by members of the ruling house, the Kulas. High offices in the state were a monopoly of the land -owning elite and had resulted in the weakening of the power of the king and neglect of the obligations of the feudatory. The latter's power to raise and maintain his own army and raise his own taxes had, by the time of invasion, led to dispersion of political authority and had encouraged centrifugal forces.

Most of the feudatories had their own feudatories like *samantas, thakurs, rawats* etc. The Rashtrakutas, for instance, had feudatories like the Gujarat Rashtrakutas and Silharas who, in turn, had sub-feudatories. In Kashmir the feudal lords lived in small castles, maintained their contingents and defied the central power as and when they pleased.[51]

The feudatories were not permitted to issue coins and they had to mention the name of the overlord in epigraphs; they had to attend the court of the overlord on ceremonial occasions; pay tribute regularly, make gifts on certain occasions and when daughters were married, and to send a number of troops when required.[52]

The large scale operations of the Ghurids in the last quarter of the 12th and first quarter of the 13th centuries were not unexpected, for the Turks had been making constant efforts to increase their area of influence in north India. According to Baihaqi, Ahmad Niyaltigin had penetrated as far as Benaras and Masud, Mahmud's son, had captured Hansi. Hindu inscriptions also tell the same tale. An inscription of Lakhanpala of Badaun mentions his ancestor, Madanpala, as making Hammira's incursion into the river of the gods (Ganges) impossible. The Sarnath inscription of Kumaradevi praises Govindachandra (1114-55) as one who had protected Benaras from the wicked Turushka warriors. The Delhi-Siwalik pillar inscription of Visaldeva dated 1164, describes the king as one who had extirpated the *mlecchas*.[53]

It is notable that at no time did the Turkish invaders face a popular uprising.[54] The rulers fought repeatedly and bravely but the society, as such, made no effort to combat the invaders through a radical reform of the social system. So convinced were the Hindus of the rightness of their social institutions that they never saw them as being, in any way, responsible for their downfall. Instead, they closed their ranks and turned inwards to guard their cherished institutions rather than facing the danger squarely and trying to combat it by finding the right solutions. But then this has been a special feature of Indian society, whether Hindu or Muslim, through the ages.[55]

Md. Habib writes "At almost any time before the accession of Alauddin Khilji, a stout Hindu attack would have brought the rickety empire of Delhi to the ground. Muslim statesmen certainly showed a greater foresight and tact than their rivals; the bitter lessons of the past had prepared them for a desperate and successful struggle against the Mongol hordes, while their comparative freedom from the trammels of custom and tradition enabled them to plan and execute the revenue reforms which the country needed. The leadership of the Hindus had fallen to the Rajputs who were too disunited and too fond of internecine warfare to combine together either for internal administration or external defence; nor was it in the desert of Rajasthan that the empire of India could be established or overthrown." [56]

He ascribes the easy conquest of India to a turnover of public opinion--one that was long overdue. According to him, the industrial and social forces of the country had long been ready for change but the rigidity of the caste barrier made any change impossible. The external pressure broke the barrier and the substitution of the old rulers by the new made it possible for the Indian workers to obtain their rights.[57]

The new rulers permitted them to live within the city walls with their families instead of leaving them outside to fend for themselves against all dangers. Those who wished could join the army as active fighters and could engage in various trades of their choice.

Meeting of two Great Religions

The Islamic and Hindu creeds seem to have been tailor made to set the followers of each on a collision course with those of the other. The stark monotheism of pure Islam cannot easily co-exist with Hindu pantheism. Though at the highest philosophical level, Hinduism also admits of only one supreme entity but its manifestations at various levels make for a colourful patheon of millions of gods that can only shock the true believer of an all- pervading invisible deity that permits no cognisance of any other power. The social structure of the two communities also created a wide schism. The rigidity of the caste system which countenanced no overstepping of social limitations imposed by birth could hardly have any comparability with Islamic democracy where all Muslims were considered equal irrespective of birth, education or wealth.

However, as Islam travelled through various areas before reaching India, many of its original teachings had been greatly eroded. Belief in omens and astrology; faith in miracles that could be worked by holy men both living and dead; the placing of the king just one rung below God; the recognition of *mullahs* as arbiters of religion; the removal of equality between Muslims, except in name, all made the religion rather far removed from the starkly simple monotheistic Islam that had originally appeared in the Arabian peninsula and had given a clarion call to primitive people to declare the oneness of God and the unity of Man.

However, the clarion call still served to arouse great emotion in the hearts of its followers. Says Aziz Ahmad, "The feeling of social equality was enshrined in the mosque and was held close to the heart of even the common soldier.The takbir, Allah-o-Akbar (God is great), made him forget his low status, the hardships of battle, the greed of his officers and any other consideration and carried him forward as an invincible force crushing everything before him. He had his consolation. In a righteous war if he killed he became a ghazi and if he died he became a shahid, martyr. In either case he was assured of either worldly or Heavenly pleasures. It was a sure fire formula for ensuring remarkable feats of bravery and endurance."

He continues, "The majority of Indians were asked to defend the temples of gods to which they had been denied entrance for generations. They refused. They were asked to maintain the power and privileges of the Kshatriyas and Brahmans by whom they had been reduced to the condition of beasts. They felt no call to die in defence of such privilege. They were asked to defend a great and sacred literature, a literature so sacred that they would be punished with death for acquiring it. Here lies the solution of the Turko-Muslim conquest of India."[58]

Inspite of these differences, however, Hindus and Muslims managed to live in amity for centuries. The Muslim armies fought hard against kings and organised armies but left the common people alone. In spite of *takbir* that provided such inspiration to the soldier the primary purpose of warfare was not conversion to Islam. As has been noted elsewhere in this work, converts were not considered equals of born Muslims and were regarded as a real threat to the power of the immigrants into the country. While in Islam conversion is considered a duty in some cases it is not prescribed as an universal norm. The Quran pragmatically states, "As for the disbelievers, whether thou warn them or thou warn them not (of the evil of their ways) it is all one for them; they believe not. Allah hath sealed their hearing and their hearts and on their eyes there is a covering. . . ."(Q2: 6, 7)

The State was undoubtadly Islamic in character and every action had to be justified in that light. The *fatehnamas*, accounts of victories, always found a religious excuse for all carnage and pillage. Since such carnage against fellow Muslims could hardly be justified in the light of *Jihad,* holy war, all sorts of allegations of apostasy were hurled against co-religionist opponents. Against non-Muslim opponents, naturally, every war was a righteous one. The *fatehnama* itself and later historians recounted with unholy glee the large numbers of casualties, the amount of plunder and other details of the campaign. Historians vied with each other in depicting kings as great crusaders of religion. According to them no wars were fought just for material gain.

If we take into account the large numbers of Hindus who were supposed to have been put to the sword or deprived of their wealth, we would find Barani's description of the prosperity of the Hindus as a mere myth, as also Feroze Shah Tughlak's description of the same. But the fact remains that even after over seven hundred years of Muslim rule 9 out of 10 Indians remained Hindu and barring few exception, Hindus were able to practice their religion with relative freedom. This can be considered a tribute not only to the Hindu genius for survival but also Muslim tolerance of non-Muslim practices.

There undoubtedly were conversions, some of which were ascribed to the Sufis, although Sufi records are silent on the subject. Others may have been due to genuine faith in the precepts of the new religion; still others may have been due to a chance for bettering of economic prospects or a final desperate attempt to throw off the shackles and injustices of caste.

In the wake of any conquest there is never a dearth of opportunists seaking to curry favour with the new rulers in every possible way. The conversion of large groups of certain castes to Islam seems to have been one such step. Perhaps the rulers would naturally be inclined to deal with co-religionists rather than with outsiders leading to additional prosperity for the converted group. These converted groups, however, never forgot their original social regulations and remained loyal to caste and other rules while taking on the precepts of the new religion. Many of them even continued to honour various deities along with Allah thus producing a Muslim culture that became unique to the subcontinent and had very little in common with Islam in other areas.

The Turks treated Hindus and neo-Muslims with equal negligence. They were more interested in maintaining their power and prestige than in acting as real bigots. There is no record of any Turkish Sultan's orders interfering with Hindu religious practices.[59] The kings were too canny to try to play the role of religious crusaders, especially in the face of such an overwhelming number of *Kafirs* with whom they were faced.

Shihabuddin Muhammad of Ghur continued to use the figure of Lakshmi on his gold coins. Kings entered into alliance with Hindu chiefs and allowed conquered rulers to continue to practice their religion and to rule according to their own laws in lieu of certain considerations.

Even in the capital, Delhi, Hindus took out religious processions, worshipped idols and bathed in the Jamuna. From archaeological reports (Journal of the United Provinces Historical Society July 1943- Cunningham, Vol. I, p. 206; Report of the Archaeological Survey of India, pp. 112-117; Reports of the Archaeological Survey of India 1909-10, p.131) it appears that temples were constructed during this period and that there was no State interference. Three images of the Jain sect discovered in Etah, U.P. contain detailed records of their installation in V.S. 1335/ 1278 A.D. A fragment of a bilingual inscription in the Purana Kila of Delhi records the endowment of 12 bighas of land for the construction of a temple dedicated to Sri Krishna.

Notes

1. M. Habib, *Politics and Society during early Medieval Period*, p. 87. Hereinafter referred to as Habib.
2. Ibid., p. 68.
3. Ibid., p. 69.
4. Ashirbadi Lal Srivastava, *The Sultanate of Delhi* (including the Arab Invasion of Sind) 711-1526 A.D., p. 33. Hereinafter referred to as Srivastava.
5. Habib, p. 68.
6. Minhaj-us-Siraj, *Tabaqat-i-Nasiri*, edited and Translated by Major H.G. Raverty. p. 85, footnote 9. Hereinafter referred to as Raverty.
7. C.E. Bosworth, *The Ghaznavids, Their Empire in Afghanistan and Eastern Iran, 944-1041*, p. 110. Hereinafter referred to as Bosworth.
8. Ibid., p. 89.
9. Elliot and Dowson, *History of India as Told by its Own Historians*, Vol. II., p. 130. Hereinafter referred to as Elliot & Dowson.
10. Ibid., p. 133.
11. Ibid., p. 133.
12. Minhaj-us-Siraj, *Tabaqat-i-Nasiri*, pp. 353-354. Hereinafter referred to as Minhaj.
13. Ibid., pp. 354-355.
14. Raverty, pp. 85-86, footnote 9.
15. Srivastava, p. 50.
16. A.B.M. Habibullah, *The Foundation of Muslim Rule in India*, p. 321.
17. Srivastava, p. 47.
18. Alberuni, *Alberuni's India*, p. viii. Hereinafter referred to as Alberuni.
19. Bosworth, pp. 131-133.
20. Alberuni, p. viii.
21. Ibid., pp. xxxiv, xxxv, xxxviii.

22. Ibid., p. xxxix.
23. Ibid., p. xxi.
24. R.C. Majumdar, H.C. Raychaudhuri & K. Datta, *An Advanced History of India*, p. 160.
25. Ibid., pp. 212-213.
26. Ibid., pp. 214-216.
27. Ibid., p. 212.
28. Alberuni, p. 163.
29. Ibid., p. 23.
30. Ibid, p. xviii.
31. Ibid., pp. 196-208.
32. Ibid., p. 171.
33. Ibid., pp. 104-105.
34. Ibid., p. 22.
35. Habib, p. 65.
36. Ibid., p. 64.
37. Ibid., p. 62.
38. Ibid., p. 64.
39. Minhaj, pp. 556-558.
40. Srivastava, p. 48.
41. Elliot & Dowson, Vol. II, with foreword by M. Habib, pp. 47-49.
42. H.K. Naqvi, *Agricultural Industrial and Urban Dynamism under the Sultans of Delhi, 1206-1555*, p. 134.
43. Bosworth, pp. 115-116.
44. Srivastava, p. 85.
45. Minhaj, pp. 467-468.
46. Srivastava, p. 73.
47. Ibid., pp. 84-85.
48. Ibid., pp. 20-21.
49. Ibid., p. 30.
50. M. Habib & K.A. Nizami (ėd), *A Comprehensive History of India*, p. 132. Hereinafter referred to as Habib and Nizami.
51. Ibid., p. 133.
52. A.S. Altekar, *The State and Government in Ancient India*, p. 225.
53. Habib & Nizami, pp. 133-137.
54. K.A. Nizami, *Some Aspects of Religion and Politics in India during the Thirteenth Century*, p. 91. Hereinafter referred to as Nizami.
55. Muhammad Aziz Ahmad, *Political History and Institutions of the early Turkish Empire of Delhi*, pp. 42-46. Hereinafter referred to as Muhammad Aziz Ahmad.
56. Habib, pp. 24-25.
57. Elliot & Dowson, Vol. II, foreword by M. Habib, pp. 55-56.
58. Muhammad Aziz Ahmad, p. 52.
59. Nizami, pp. 320-321.

9

THE SUFI AND THE ULEMA

Sufis

No record of the early period of Indian medieval history can be complete without reference to the role played by the Sufis in the consolidation of the Turkish empire in Delhi.

Sufism, the mystical branch of Islam, started in Iraq during the Umayyad period mostly in Kufa and Basra. Its followers were men of deep religious feelings and belonged mostly to the conquered communities. By the 12th century there were 12 schools of mystics with distinct beliefs--those who believed in reincarnation; those who declared "I am the Truth"; those who believed in *Fana*, annihilation of the self in God and so on. Even the doctrine of Nirvana was postulated by the founder of one of the schools, "If a man turns himself towards Allah and attaches himself to Allah, and forgets his own existence and forgets everything except Allah--then if you ask him, 'wherefrom are you and what object do you desire he will have no answer but Allah".[1]

The Silsilahs

The foundations of the *Silsilahs* or mystic orders in the 13th century followed the consolidation of mystic thought.[2]

The *Sheikh* of the *Silsilah* was one to whom his *guru* or teacher had given the *Khilafat namah* or certificate of succession. This could be any qualified disciple who could then be sent anywhere in the world to propagate the precepts of the faith. The disciple in turn became a Sheikh and chose his own followers.[3]

The *Silsilahs*, however, frequently quarrelled with each other and even among the followers of the same *Silsilah* there was no coordination.

There could, thus, be no possibility of the setting up of an international hierarchy as strong as, say, the Catholic Church.[4]

Of the many mystic orders started in the 12th century, and active even today, the two most influential during the Sultanate period were the Chistia and the Suhrawardia, started respectively by Muinuddin Chisti at Ajmer, and Bahauddin Zakariya at Multan. While the latter remained confined to the Punjab, the former spread all over India. Muinuddin was considered a saint of the highest merit and his presence near the King is said by Minhaj to have enabled Muhammad Ghuri to conquer Ajmer. Muinuddin died in Ajmer in 1235 and his tomb has since become the most holy Islamic shrine in India visited by king and commoner alike. Tombs of other *Mashaik* (plural of Sheikh), as the outstanding mystics were titled, also became places of pilgrimage such as the tomb of Qutabuddin Bakhtiyar Kaki and Nizamuddin Aulia at Delhi and others in different parts of the country.

The worshipof the Muslim saint and his shrine arose out of reverence by the Muslims but also owed a great deal to the Hindu reverence for anyone or anything showing signs of super-natural power. It was the simplicity and humanism of the Sufi that gained Islam a large number of converts. At the behest of his teacher the pupil travelled great distances and settled in different parts of the country such as Bengal and Gujarat, in humble surroundings among the local people, learned their language and through sympathyand identification with them, drew them to himself like a magnet. His mysticism may not have been identical to that of Hindu Vedantism but it certainly provided a point of contact between followers of the two faiths.[5]

The Bhakti movement, teaching that love formed the relationship between man and God and that serving God with devotion was better than indulging in rituals and ceremonies, was a common creed to both the Bhakt and the Sufi who respected each other and found followers in both religions. Music was common to both since it was through this strong medium that the common man learnt the creed of love and harmony while experiencing a sense of religious ecstasy.

The Sufis on their part, were always eager to establish links with the Hindus and learn about their religion. It is significant that their maximum contact was with leaders of the Bhakti cult like Nanak, Kabir, Chaitanya etc. who all belonged to the lower classes and had spent some time in the *khanqahs* of the Sufis.

The Sufis exhorted their Muslim disciples to look with sympathy and understanding on the Hindus "Oh you who sneer at the idolatry of the Hindu/Learn also from him how worship is done." "Though the Hindu is not faithful like me. He often believes in the same things as I do" declared Amir Khusrau.[6] In another place he wrote, "Every people has its tolerant (legitimate) path, its religion and its temple.[7]

Music and language together played an important part in bringing the two people closer. Though, Sanskrit remained the language of higher learning, regional languages also began to develop enough to have good translations of the classics which were now available to people knowing Tamil, Telugu, Persian, Arabic etc.

A number of original works also came into being such as the *Haravilasa*, a number of poems in praise of Siva composed by the Telugu poet Srinadha, and the *Padmavat* of Malik Muhammad Jayasi in Hindi. The genius of Amir Khusrau, the inventor of new musical instruments and *ragas* and a poet of the calibre of the highest ranking Persian poets, not only wrote poetry in the local language, but managed to combine the choicest Persian and Hindi words and phrases in the same poem without lessening either the quality of the poem or detracting in any way from the full meaning of the phrases.

The mystics lived mostly in cities--Baba Farid at Ajodhan, now in Pakistan, Saiyed Muhammad Bandenawaz Gesudaraz at Gulbarga, Shah Alam Bukhari at Gujrat, Bahauddin Zakariya at Sylhet but they avoided court rituals and managed not only to retain their independence in the face of autocratic monarchs but forced many of the latter to visit them in their humble abodes and submit to their will.

The conquerors made little impact on the rural population but those Muslims who went to live in villages adopted the customs of the area and became almost indistinguishable from the local population. One of the disciples of Muinuddin Chisti, Sheik Hamiduddin, lived the life of a peasant in Suwal, a small village in Nagaur. Like the rest of the villagers he produced all the food and clothes he needed for his own use, lived in a small mud house and cultivated a single bigha of land. He kept a single cow which he milked himself, and was a strict vegetarian and forbade his disciples to distribute meat dishes after his death. He dressed like a Hindu peasant with two pieces of cloth, one covering the upper and the second the lower part of his body. He insisted that in his household only Hindi, the local language, be spoken. Since the rotation of crops was not known in India he cultivated half his land in one season and the other half in the next. His life at Nagaur offers one of the earliest glimpses of family life in the Indian countryside.

One point on which the Sufis firmly opposed authority was the propagation of education. The govering classes were opposed to dissemmination of education among the lower classes since that would blur the clear cut distinction between them and the élite. The Sufis, on the other hand, fought doggedly against caste distinction and also against illiteracy. Visitors to the *Khanqahs* were treated with strict equality whether they were kings or beggars. Theirs, by and large, was a separate world uncontaminated by considerations of power and wealth.[8]

Urban Bias

Muslims have basically been urban rather than rural minded. The Arabic word for city and civilisation (*madina, tamaddun, madaniyat*) has the same root. This, perhaps, derives from the fact that in Arabia culture could flourish only in cities. All the social requisites such as small mosques for daily prayers and children's education; larger ones for congregational prayers and higher learning and charitable institutions for looking after the poor were all situated in cities.Keeping in mind the difficulty of bringing the nomadic people under a rigid discipline, the Quran itself instructed the nomadic tribes to call themselves Musalmans rather than the Mumins (believers). Since their entry into the fold of Islam had been a mere formality the *mullahs* decreed that for the salvation of the villager or nomadic people under a rigid discipline the Quran itself intructed the nomadic tribe it was enough just to be able to recite the *Kalimah*, the Muslim affirmation of faith (There is no God but Allah and Muhammad is his Prophet).

Because of the importance of the city it had a special place in Muslim cultrure and historians named most states after their capitals, including the Sultanate (empire) of Delhi. Naturally, therefore, the *Khanqahs* of the Sufis were also situated in cities.[9]

The *Khanqahs* permitted no religious discussion, the conversation being strictly limited to mystical matters.

Shunning of Honours

Almost all the mystic saints of India, especially the Chistis, followed the earlier tradition of Muslim mystics of shunning kings and courtiers. Khwaja Qutbuddin Bakhtiyar visited the court of Iltutmish only once while Shaikh Fariduddin Gang-i-Shakar told his disciples "If you desire to attain the position of great saints do not pay any attention to the princes." They refused jagirs and endowments of land or money.

Nizamuddin Auliya's injunctions to his disciples were couched in no uncertain terms "Do not accept any village or stipend or favour from kings and officials. It is not permitted to a dervish." Sheikh Farid was so keen to get rid of large sum of money sent to him by Balban that although it was quite dark by the time the gift was received he had it immediately distributed among the poor saying that his *Khanqah* was not a storehouse for royal gifts.

Shaikh Qutbuddin Bakhtiyar Kaki refused to accept the title of Shaikh-ul-Islam that Iltutmish sought to bestow on him while another mystic, Shaikh Hasan pretended to turn mad to evade his appointment as Qazi. When Bakhtiyar Kaki heard of this derangement he said "Shaikh Hasan is not mad, he is wise (dana)," Thus it was that Shaikh Hasan had the suffix Dana added to his name.[10]

These restrictions against acquisition of earthly goods and honours were placed on the high grade of mystics who had received the Khilafat namah or patent of spiritual authority by their preceptor. Those,not in the same category, were however,not bound by the same precepts of asceticism. Thus Amir Khusrau, one of the most favourite disciples of Nizamuddin Auliya, was allowed to live a normal urban life along with his mystic one. He consorted with kings and nobles and held high offices in courts and camps.

Means of Livelihood

Two means of livelihood were premitted to the sufis--*thya*--cultivation of waste land, and*futuh*---unasked for charity. According to Muslim jurists,waste land becomes the property of those who develop it. The Quran states that the basic necessities of life, like food and water (*Rizq-i-mazmun*), are supplied by God to all living creatures and since a mystic's needs should conform strictly to these necessities there was no need to strive for further worldly benefits. Sheikh Nasiruddin Chirag is said to have stated very clearly the Chisti point of view on the subject. "There are two disciplines--one prescribed for the initiated and the other for the novices. For the select few, the injunction was to shut their doors and pray to God; for the general run of men the instruction was to go out and earn a livelihood by dint of labour." However, on no account, must they eat their religion. In other words, piety should not be exploited for worldly ends or to avoid labour.[11]

To the *sufi* the solving of the problems of the poor was as important as offering prayers to God. According to Shaikh Farid, "There can be no pleasure in devotions so long as there remains a single needy person at the door."[12]

Nizamuddin Auliya always told his audience, "No one in the world has a sadness and sorrow like me. So many people come and tell me about their troubles and worries and everything gets impressed upon my heart and soul."[3]

Suhrawardis

These above restrictions were rigidly applied to the Chisti *Silsilah*. In contrast, the Suhrawardi *Silsilah* consorted with kings though mainly to persuade them to change their ways and be able to redress wrongs done to certain persons. Najubuddin Abdur Qadir Suhrawardi exhorted his disciples to be reverent towards rulers and not to find tfault with them. Another saint of the same order, Saiyyid Jalauddin Bukhari, at one time declared that rulers are chosen by God and on no account must disrespect be shown to them or their order disobeyed. On another occasion, however, he stated that it was abominable to eat the food of maliks and Sultans since their revenue was mostly derived from sources based on tyranny and oppression.[14]

The Suhrawardis were also in favour of mystics hoarding wealth and living in style. They also dabbled in politics. Shaikh Bahauddin Zakariya, though living in Qabacha's domain, supported Iltutmish in extending his power and authority, and wrote a letter to him which was intercepted by Qabacha. Being unable to touch the mystic because of his great popularity with the people of Multan, Qabacha punished the Qazi instead by accusing him of treason and putting him to death.[15]

In the hurly burly of 13th century India, amidst the clash of arms, the trampling feet of war elephants, the sound of the soliders' marching feet up and down north India, the *Khanqahs* of the mystics provided examples of deep stillness, piety and humanitarian causes.

The mystics strove for communion with God but their asceticism did not include celibacy. Except for certain religious exercises, designed to bring about a particular mystic experience they led a life no different from that of the common man. They married, had children and maintained a regular household.[16]

The sufis were prolific writers. They helped, by mixing completely with the local population, in developing a composite culture. Their literature is full of accounts of mutual exchange of ideas, dietary habits and cultural patterns with the local population. They condoned, as has been earlier, idol worship, vegetarianism and other local practices.

Shaikh Fariduddin Ganj-i-shakar, Shaikh Nizamuddin Aulia, Shaikh Nasiruddin Chirag and Qazi Hamid Nagauri were, apart from being great mystics, powerful writers. So great was the popular hunger for mystic writing that it gave rise to enormous quantities of spurious literature being produced in the great men's name and available in large quantities in the *bazaars*. In spite of the denial of authorship by the supposed authors the literature never lacked buyers.[17]

The *sufis*, though unconventional and often even maverick, were staunch Muslims. They meticulously observed the injunctions for prayer and fasting and saw their way as the true path to piety and truth (*Haqiqat*). However, as has been seen they shunned politics and worldly honours. No theocratic state could, naturally, function under their guidance. So a whole set of ecclesiastics were trained to, so to speak, keep the State on the path of righteousness as shown by the Faith, to lay down religious laws, to interpret doctrines, settle disputes and carry out the myriad duties required for the State to function. They formed the religious establishment and were known as the *Ulema*.

The Shias

Most of the Turkish *maliks* were slaves and few had been born into Islam. They were converted to *Sunni* Islam which was the state religion. To be a *Shia* was politically dangerous, since adherence to the sect involved allegiance to the enemies of the *Abbasides* whose recognition gave the Delhi Sultan his legitimacy. They were denounced as heretics and were designated *mulahidah* and *rawafiz*. They were persecuted everywhere and their headquarters in northern Iran became the target of a series of attacks by different tribes. Hunted and terrorised, they became a secret society and in turn, terrorised Sunnis through *fidais* or fanatic adherents, who became expert assassins. It was only after the conversion of the Il-Khans of Iran to Shia-ism that the sect received political sanction.

In India only in Sind, which was Arab ruled, an extremist sect of the Ismailis, the *Qaramitah*, won political power in upper Sind. In Multan amd Mansur for more than 2 centuries allegiance was owed to the *Fatemid* caliphs of Egypt. Muhammad Ghuri had to fight hard to overthrow the *Qaramitahs* and his death at their hands made the Turks bitterly hostile to them.[18]

The Ulema

The *Ulema* constituted a very influential section of Muslim society in the middle ages. They were revered for their learning and were considered heirs to the Prophet. Anyone who acquired a high degree of knowledge could become an "*alim*", but his renown and popularity depended on his piety and devotion to the cause of knowledge. He was expected to be well versed in *ilm-i-faraiz* (knowledge of the rights and duties of a Muslim) so that he could help people to regulate their lives according to the laws of the *Shariat*. A man who became a savant just for the sake of earning money lost his prestige and was generally looked down upon.

After the completion of his education an *alim* had many avenues open to him. He could decide to lead a life of austere piety cut off from wordly affairs or he could choose to go into various professions. He could become a teacher, holding classes in his own house or a mosque. Those who taught in *madrassahs* established by the Sultan were highly paid and respected. Ambitious men could become *qazis, muftis, imams, khatibs, mahtasibs* rising to such high posts as ambassadors, *sadr-i-jahan, sadr-us-sudur or Shaikh-ul-Islam.* They were known as *danish-mand*, wise.[19]

Some of the scholars were appointed as *muzakkirs* who delivered discourses on an average 3 times a week and everyday during the months of *Ramzan, Muharram* and *Zil-Hijjah.*

Naturally, in spite of their show of piety and learning each of the *ulema* differed in character and even morality. Shaikh Jamaluddin Bistami, one of the *Shaikh-ul-Islam* during the reign of Iltutmish, was a man of great learning and piety while Najmuddin Sughra was vain and unscrupulous. He was extremely jealous of anyone who could be a possible competitor and let no opportunity pass to run them down in the eyes of the King.[20] As opposed to this, Maulana Nur Turk, an ascetic and learned theoligion, famous for his reverence and piety, hated his fellow theologians for their materialistic pursuits and criticised them publicly. He himself spent only one *dang* a day given to him by his freed slave. Once Raziya sent him a bag of of gold. Enraged, he beat the bag with a stick and told the messenger to remove it from his sight.[21]

Qazis

Shaikh Jalal-ud-din Tabrizi told the Qazi of Badaun " The great ambition of the *Ulema* is to become a *mutawali* or teacher somewhere. If they aspire for something higher it is *qaziship* of some town. Their highest ambition is the office of *Sadr-i-jahan*. Beyond that they dare not aspire for anything."[22]

Qazis were mainly concerned with civil disputes and their appointment was considered a matter of high priority in every town.[3] Nizami mentions the names of 25 *qazis* including Minhaj. He quotes Balban as saying, "I have three qazis... Fakhr-i-Naqila fears me but does not fear God; the Qazi-i-Lashkar fears God but does not fear me; Minhaj neither fears me nor God." It was to the King's credit that he most respected the *Qazi-i-Lashkar* who feared God rather than the King and respected his recommendations.[24]

Qazis were mainly concerned with civil disputes, other matters being under the jurisdiction of the *Diwan-i-Mazalim* and the *Diwan-i-Siyasat* who were purely secular in character, neither being assigned to run according to the laws of the *Shariat*. The general attitude of the Muslim community was summed up in a remark, "The *Qazi* is for the evil-doers; what has he to do with good people?" Nizamuddin Aulia's reply to Shaikh Najibuddin Mutawakkil's request to pray for his appoi-ntment to the post of *Qazi* reflects the same attitude "Don't be *Qazi* be something else."[25]

However, *Qazis* could not always act on their initiative without obtaining a *fatwa*, edict, from the *Ulema*.[26]

In the inevitable dispute between the Sufis and the *Ulema* the latter, much as they might disapprove of the unorthodox behaviour of the former could not take unilateral measures. Minhaj-us-Siraj legalised the institution of *Sama* (mystic music) and the step was not reversed even when two *qazis* requested Iltutmish to convene a gathering of the *Ulema* to consider the legality of the action.

A qazi of Ajodhan who did not approve of the goings-on at Shaikh Farid's gatherings brought up the question in a round-about way to the scholars of Multan. He described the Shaikh as an educated man who lives in a mosque, hears songs and dances and asked the ulema's opinion on such goings-on. When pressed to reveal the identity of the person concerned he was told, " You have referred to saint against whom no *mujtahid* dare raise his finger." so enraged was the Qazi at this verdict, that he seriously contemplated hiring an assassin to kill the Shaikh.[27]

Khatibs and Imams

A learned theological scholar could look forward to being appointed *Khatib* or *Imam*. But really such posts went only to people who were known for their learning and were well-read though there were some exceptions. When Maulana Malik Yar was appointed Imam of the Badaun mosque there was an uproar because he lacked formal education. The leading scholar of the city, Alauddin Usuli, defended the step saying that because of his exceptional spiritual qualities, "Even if the *imamat* of the Friday mosque of Baghdad was entrusted to Maulana Malik Yar, it would be nothing compared to his abilities."[28]

The *Khatibs* and *Imams*, by and large, led very prosperous lives. Some, with exceptional powers of eloquence, were appointed *muzakkirs* who delivered sermons during the month of *Ramzan* and recited the tragic happenings at Karbala during the month of *Muharram.* On special occasions, such as the eve of battle, they were called upon to harangue the people and arouse in them the required sentiment of loyalty, patriotism, subjection etc.

Minhaj who held all offices including *Qazi, Khatib, Imam* and was considered an authority on the *Shariat* was an outstanding preacher. Shaikh Nizamuddin Auliya who attended his meetings every Monday, was on one occasion, so moved that for a while he lost all consciousness of his surroundings.[29]

Minhaj himself recounts that he preached 95 times before the king in the matter of a few months.[30]

The *ulema* were a force to be reckoned with but in a political rather than religious sense. Their influence over the people was considerable and their alliance was sought by both rebels and the establishment. They were thus wooed by both sides and were always treated with respect.

It seemed to be a case of mutual aid and admiration. The *Ulema*, from all evidence, condoned the activities of the kings who treated them well. There is no record of edicts against kings who failed to offer prayers or fast during *Ramzan*. Even wine drinking was condoned as a fit indulgence of kings. Iltutmish was, therefore, always very careful not to do anything to irritate them. Even though he did not always follow their wishes, his handling of them was so astute that he made them powerful allies and so strengthened his position as king.[31]

The *masjid* (mosque), the *madrasah* (school), the *maqbara* (tomb) were all centres of religious activity. Mosques, though used mostly for congregational prayers, doubled as schools and a number of ceremonies were performed there.

Mausoleums

Mausoleums were centres of brisk activity. Ibn Batuta records in the *Rehla* that 460 persons were employed at the tomb of Sultan Qutbuddin Mubarak Shah to perform different services. "I appointed", he says, "one hundred and fifty reciters of the Quran who are known as *Khatmi*; eighty students; eight repeaters called *mukarrarin,* one professor and eighty *sufis*; and I appointed an *Imam*, muezzins, pleasant voiced readers and clerks who might register the absentees as well as ushers. All these people in this country are known as *arbab*. Further, I appointed another class of functionaries known as domestic (*hashia*), namely the valets, the cooks, the running footmen (*davadavia*), the water bears (*abdariya,* that is the *saqqaun*), the *sherbat* dispensers, the betel givers, the arms-bearers, the spear-bearers, the umbrella bearers, the laver, carriers, the chamberlains and the heralds--all these numbering four hundred and sixty.... on the occasion of the great festivals, the two Ids, the birthday of the Prophet, the 10th of Muharram (Ashura), the night of mid-Shaban and the day of Sultan Qutubuddin's death--I used a hundred maunds of flour and an equal amount of meat with which I fed the poor and indigent." He adds, "It is a custom among the Indians to provide for their dead in the same way as they do during their lifetime. They bring elephants and horses and tie them near its gate and the tomb is highly decorated." [32]

The graves of saints and Sultans were used by people to swear an oath of allegiance or to make a vow. The *sufis* had the dastar (turban) tied to their heads, to indicate their rise to a position of eminence at the graves ofwell known mystics.[33]

Balban's grave had a special significance. He had built a house of safety *Dar-ul-Aamm.* A debtor who entered it had his debt paid by the Sultan. The Sultan himself interceded with the heirs of the deceased when a murderer sought refuge in the house. The pursuers of any criminal entering the house were offered satisfaction. Balban himself was later buried in the house.[34]

Religion vs. Science

The *Ulema*, as has been seen above, were well-vertsed in *ilm-i-faraiz* (rights and duties) of a Muslim but their fundamentally religious out look narrowed their vision and, in the process, scientific development came to standstill. Science had been borrowed by the Muslims from the

Greeks and Hindus and up to about the 10th century flourished greatly. Later, however, it came into conflict with orthodoxy and became stagnant. Alberuni and Shaikh Bu Ali Sina were the last great Muslim scientists. Mahmud of Ghazni, trying to make the *ulema* his allies, started persecuting scientists. The two above-mentioned scientists were brought to Ghazni when the Sultan raided their homeland. Bu Ali Sina managed to escape but his great treatise on medicine became the Bible of Muslim physicians and any deviation from it came to be looked on almost a heresy. Alberuni came to India with the Sultan and, among his other works, wrote the first description of Indian society. Mahmud even persecuted the Ismailis in Sind who were inclined towards science and is said to have ordered their hands and feet to be cut off.[35]

Alberuni, himself a scientist of repute, and never afraid to express his views, wrote, " The number of sciences is great and it may still be greater if the public mind is directed towards them at such times as they are in the ascendency and in general favour with all, when people honour not only science itself but also its representatives. To do this is, in the first instance, the duty of those who rule over them, of kings and princes. For they alone could free the mind of scholars from their daily anxieties of the necessities of life and stimulate their energies to earn more fame and favour, the yearning for which is the pith and marrow of human nature. The present times, however, are not of this kind. They are the very opposite and, therefore, it is impossible that a new science or a new kind of research should arise in our days. What we have of science is nothing but the scanty remains of bygone better times." As Hindu scientific thought had been stagnant for centuries, so he prophesied would be the future of Muslim science.

Fortunately, literature and the arts, with the exception of painting, were allowed to prosper and flourish. Painting was forbidden since the images created could lead to idol sworship and painter was said to be "rivalling God". The Mongol rulers of Persia, the 11 Khans, fortunately ignored Muslim opinion and patronised painting until the Muslim *Ulema* finally came to accept it.[36]

Notes

1. M. Habib, *Politics and Society during the early Medieval Period*, pp. 52-53. Hereinafter referred to as Habib.
2. Ibid., p. 54.
3. Ibid., p. 55.
4. Ibid., p. 56.

5. A.B.M. Habibullah, *The Foundation of Muslim Rule in India*, pp. 303-307. Hereinafter referred to as Habibullah.
6. Shirin Khusrau, *Amir Khusrau*, Text edited by Haj Ali Ahmed Khan.
7. Habib, p. 21.
8. K.A. Nizami, *Some Aspects of Religion and Politics in India during the Thirteenth Century*, pp. 186-262. Hereinafter referred to as Nizami.
9. Habib, p. 36.
10. Nizami, p. 245.
11. Khair-ul-Majalis: *Conversations of Shaikh Nasir-ud-Din Chirag of Delhi* compiled by Hamid Qalandar. Text edited by K.A.Nizami, p. 80. Hereinafter refered to as Khair-ul-Majalis.
12. Nizami, p. 206.
13. Khair-ul-Majalis, op. cit., p. 105.
14. Nizami, pp. 249-251.
15. Fawaid-ul-Fuad, *Conversations of Sheikh Nasir-ud-Din Auliya*, compiled by Amir Ali Sijzi.
16. Habibullah, pp. 304-306.
17. M. Habib and Afsar Usman Salim Khan, *The Political Theory of the Delhi Sultanate* (including a translation of Zia-ul-Din Barani's *Fatawa-i-Jahandari* circa 1358-9 A.D.), p. iii.
18. Habibullah, pp. 301-305.
19. Nizami, pp. 151-152.
20. Ibid., p. 162.
21. Fawaid-ul-Fuad, p. 199..
22. Siyar-ul-Aulya, *Saiyyid Muhammed b. Mubarak Kirmani Known as Amir or Mirkhand.*
23. I.H. Qureshi, *Administration of the Sultanate of Delhi*, p. 152.
24. Nizami, p. 166.
25. Ibid., p. 164.
26. Ibid., p. 168.
27. Ibid., p. 168.
28. Ibid., p. 168.
29. Ibid., p. 169.
30. Minhaj us-Siraj, *Tabaqat-i-Nasiri*, p.175.
31. Nizami, p. 172.
32. Ibn Batuta, *The Rehla*, p. 36. Hereinafter referred to as Batuta.
33. Nizami, p. 305.
34. Ibn Batuta, p. 36.
35. Habib, pp. 57-58.
36. Ibid., p. 58.

10

SUMMING UP

Assessment of Raziya

Raziya was a lady endowed with remarkable talent. Minhaj writes about her, "Sultan Raziya may she rest in peace! -- was a great sovereign and sagacious, just, beneficent, the patron of the learned, a dispenser of justice, the cherisher of her subjects and of warlike talent, and was endowed with all the attributes and qualifications necessary for kings; but, as she did not attain her destiny, in her creation, of being computed among men, of what advantage were all these excellent qualifications unto her ?"[1] Farishta writes, "Ruzeea Begum was possessed of every good quality which usually adorns the ablest princes, and those who scrutinise her actions most severely will find no fault but that she was a woman. She read the Koran with the correct pronunciation and, in her father's lifetime, employed herself frequently in the affairs of the governmet, a disposition which he rather encouraged in her than otherwise." He goes on to speak of her being named her father's lifetime, employed herself frequently in the affairs of the government, a disposition which he rather encouraged in her than otherwise." He goes on to speak of her being named her father's heir because the latter said, she "though a woman had a man's head and heart and was better than 20 such sons."[2]

However, a study of Raziya's reign gives no indication of the fact that her sex was any real handicap to her. Two of her brothers, one preceding and one succeeding her, fared much worse than she did and lasted for a lesser time than her. She suffered not because of her gender, but because she was determined to curb the power of the Turkish nobles who had become king makers and were constantly intriguing to keep themselves predominant, and were therefore opposed to any sovereign, male or female, who was in any position to threaten their power. Iltutmish lasted because of his even temper and the fact that he never made a show of supremacy. In fact, in the eyes of his peers his greatest quality must have been his diffidence in their presence.

Raziya, on the other hand, acted and behaved like a sovereign. The "favour" shown to Yakut, which was made much of by later historians, amounted to nothing more than trying to counter the power of the arrogant *Maliks*. Certainly Minhaj never makes the faintest sugestion of any impropriety between her and the Ethiopian. Later historians, who felt that no woman could remain unmarried and immune to male attraction, created such a lasting myth of romance between the mistress and the slave, that even today when Raziya's name is mentioned the response is automatic. " She had an affair with Yakut."

Thomas says, "It was not that a virgin queen was forbidded to love--she might have indulged herself in a submissive Prince Consort, or revelled almost unchecked in the dark recesses of the palace harem--but wayward fancy pointed in a wrong direction and led her to prefer a person employed about her court, an Abyssinian moreover, the favours extended to whom, the Turkish nobles resented with one accord."[3]

Farishta & Badauni have said that when she mounted an elephant or horse she leaned upon yakut. The Tabakat-i-Akbari says that when she mounted for riding, the Master of the Horse who had become Amir-ul-Umra (such an office did not exist in those days) used to help her mount by taking her under the armpit, meaning, perhaps that she leant on his arm or shoulder in mounting. It could have been the routine duty and privilege of the *Amir-i-Akhur* to help the sovereign mount. No reference to any such thing is however made by Minhaj.

Elphinston, however, says "But her talents and virtues were not sufficient to protect her from a single weakness. It was shown in the extraordinary marks of favour (these are not specified) which she showed on her Master of the Horse; who, to make her partially more degrading, was an Abyssinian slave. (but had not all the Maliks started as slaves?). It does not appear that her fondness was criminal since the greatest breach of decorum alleged against her is her allowing the Abyssinian to lift her on her horse." Interestingly enough however, records show that Raziya never rode a horse, always an elephant.[4]

Her coming out of *purdah* could have been a shock to the Muslim sense of decorum, but purdah was only loosely observed until the Mongol invasion when girls and women were mercilessly raped and taken into slavery. After that it became more rigid. And, after all, even before ascending as queen she had 'shown herself' at the Friday mosque appealing to the people to give her a chance to prove her worth as their sovereign. So it can be assumed that she observed *purdah* only in name.

Sultan Raziya's reign may have been short and turbulent but it was notable in many respects. Instead of being handicapped on account of her sex Raziya's rule set many precedents:-

She was the only woman ever to become a ruler in India in her own right. That is, she did not replace a deceased husband or proxy as regent for a son or nephew. She was not a queen, but a crowned king and was therefore styled Sultan and not Sultana.

She was ignored by the nobles after her father's death, none of them honouring his wish that she should ascend the throne after his death. However, she took the matter into her own hands and fought for her right, not on the battlefield but through the people of Delhi, appealing to their sentiments and arousing their sympathies in her own favour. She, thus, became a democratically elected monarch--one of the great wonders of that age.

For the first time in the history of the Delhi Sultanate the people of Delhi decided a succession issue on their own initiative, ignoring Mahmud of Ghazni's injunction that subjects should be mere bystanders watching the deeds of kings, and never participants. She always had the people's support and, as long as she remained in capital, no revolution could succeed against her. Moreover, she promised her subjects that if she did not fulfil their expectations they were free to depose her. In that way her rule was contractual.

Raziya's independent nature was perhaps a product of her race. Turkish woman had perforce to be efficient and strong. Living as they did totally segregated from their men (see Appendix on Turks) they had, naturally, to attend to all their affairs themselves without any kind of dependence on menfolk. The Iranians also had had women rulers. Koyna Khatun and Safia Khatun were rulers of Halb while Shajarat-ul-Durr was the Turkish queen of Egypt, in the same century as Raziya ruled her empire in India. It was a credit to the opoen mindedness of the people of Delhi that they chose a woman leader and elevated her to the throne.[5]

Raziya's accession also shattered the myth of the lowly position of women in Islam. The Turks, of course, were only newly converted to Islam and, therefore, followed many of their tribal customs but there was not a single protest from the ecclesiastical community over the coming of a woman ruler on the plea of it being contrary to the precepts of Islam.

Coming to the throne, as she did without the help of the Forty, powerful Turkish nobles who had emerged as king makers freed Raziya from the constraint of feeling obligated to them or being, in any way, afraid of them. She had seen the manner in which her father and brother, or rather her step-mother had behaved towards them, always being deferential and heaping favours on them to keep them on their side and she now felt strong enough to go her own way and show favour to nonTurks in an effort to curb their arrogance and power. Her lack of success in this direction was due to causes that were in no way related to her sex. The nobles, resented her not because of her sex but because she had managed to outmanoeuvre them, reaching the throne on her own, while they were still engaged in trying to defeat her brother. Ultimately she failed not because of being a woman, but because the powerful provincial governors had no hand in her elevation to the throne, which was brought about by the central army, officers and the citizens of Delhi. Being thus deprived of their role as king makers the powerful Turkish coterie felt humiliated and ignored and became bent on bringing about her downfall.[6] Rather, it was to Raziya's great credit and a tribute to her powers of statesmanship that she managed to stay on the throne as long as she did, rather than a discredit to her that her reign was so short.

An interesting effect of the fact of Raziya's gender is the way she has been dealt with by Minhaj. Apart from the fact that she was Iltutimish's eldest daughter we have very little information about her. Other *amirs* are described according to their physical appearance. Taj-ud-Din Yalduz was "mild, beneficient, of good disposition and very handsome." Qutb-ud-Din Aibak "possessed no outward comeliness and the little finger of one hand had a fracture." Iltutmish was endowed with "comeliness, intelligence and goodness of disposition to a great degree."[7]

In the case of Raziya, however, her physical appearance is naver elaborated upon. Was she tall or short? Was she amazonian in proportions or slightly built? Did she have any physical defect? Was she autocratic and domineering or soft spoken and of a pleasant disposition? We know all her qualities as a public figure but none as a person. Even her marriage is a bit of a mystery. Firstly, why was she not married off at an early age? Did she rebel at the idea of being a mere wife and mother? Did her father find her so valuable to have at his side that he did not see her as a mere daughter but as a person in her own right capable of a great destiny? No word is forthcoming from the scribe on any of these questions. Even about her marriage to Altuniah, Minhaj simply makes the bald statement that the *Malik* entered into a matrimonial contract with her and espoused her.[8] There is no speculation about the cause of the marriage. It certainly could not have been a marriage of passion--there was no time for romance to blossom. It was obviously a political alliance, with marriage the only viable measure, to allow two people of opposite sexes to be able to move freely together without giving rise to scandal. Perhaps each of the couple entered into the matrimonial bond hoping to use the other as a stepping-stone to power. Altuniah, by marrying the Sultan, could lay claim to the throne as his right and Raziya, using his prestige, valour and military strength, had a good chance of regaining her throne.

As noted above Raziya was a ruler chosen by citizens of Delhi -Hindus and Muslims- the latter not many in number. She ruled as one of them.

According to Dr. Tara Chand ,"The Muslims who came into India made it their home. They lived surrounded by the Hindu people and a state of perennial hostility with them was impossible. Mutual intercourse led to mutual understanding. Many who had left their faith differed little from those whom they had left. " He continues, "When Qutbuddin Aibek decided to stay in Hindustan he had no other choice but to retain the Hindu staff which was familiar with the Hindu administration, for without it all government, including the collection of revenue would have fallen into utter chaos. The Muslims did not bring with them from across the frontier, any accountants and clerks. Their buildings were erected by Hindus who adapted their ancient rules to new conditions, their coins were struck by Hindu goldsmiths and their accounts were kept by Hindu officers. Brahman legislators advised the king on the administration of Hindu law and Brahman astrologers helped in the performance of their general functions."[9]

The Muslims, like so many conquerers before them also became largely Hinduised. The caste system was adopted to such an extent that there were different graveyards for different castes. Firoz Shah Tughlak provided dowry for Muslim orphan girls--a system unknown to pure Islam. Certain Indian phenomena could be expressed only in local terms and Barani consistently uses the word *barshkal* for the rainy season. Muslims, even of high born Turkish descent, adopted Indian names such as Chhajju, Kanchan, Hamidraja etc.[10]

The re-marriage of Muslim widows and divorcees came to be frowned upon--a distinct mark of the Hinduisation of Islam. One thing on which both Hindu and Muslim kings seem to have been in singular agreement was a general distrust of their sons. Writes Kautilya, "Ever since the birth of princes the king shall take special care of them." For, says Bharadwaja, "princes, like crabs, have a notorious tendency of eating up their begetter. When they are lacking in filial affections, they shall better be punished in secret." According to him, another sage advocates their being kept under the custody of boundary guards or inside a fort.[11] Muslim law having made no provision for primogeniture, fratricidal wars between aspiring heirs are a recurring event of Islamic history. A prince impatient to get his due, would not hesitate to even imprison his own father and take over the throne as was the case with Aurangzeb who kept his father in custody for eight years.[12]

Notes

1. Minhaj-us-Siraj, *Tahaqat-i-Nasiri*, pp. 637-638. Hereinafter refered to as Minhaj.
2. Mahomed Kasim Ferishta, *History of the Rise of the Mahomedan Power in India* vol I, p. 121.
3. Minhaj-us-Siraj, *Tabaqat-i-Nasiri*, edited and translated by Major H.G. Raverty. p. 642, footnote 3.
4. Ibid., pp. 642-643, footnote 3.
5. M. Habib & K.A. Nizami, *A Comprehensive History of India*, Vol.5 p. 230.
6. Ibid., pp. 237-238.
7. Minhaj pp. 499, 513, 599.
8. Ibid, p. 647.
9. Tara Chand, *Influence of Islam on Inidan Culture*, p. 137.
10. A.B.M. Habibullah: *The Foundation of Muslim Rule in India*, p.312.
11. M. Shamasastry, *Kautilya's Arthshastra*, p. 32.
12. Bamber Gascoign, *The Great Mughuls*, p. 220.

APPENDIX

THE TURKS

Whatever the nomenclature bestowed on the first Muslim dynasty to rule India, especially by western historians, contemporary records name them as Muizzi, Qutabi, Shamsi and Balbani after the names of outstanding kings i.e. Muizuddin Muhammad bin Sam, Qutbuddin Aibak, Shamsuddin Iltutmish and Ghiyasuddin Balban, whose slaves they had originally been.

The kings were Turks. They came from Turkistan, an area bounded on the *east* by China, on the *west* by Rum and on the *north* by the walls of Yajuj and Majuj (Gog & Magog) and on the *south* by the mountains of Hindustan.[1]

The tribes from which these kings originated knew reading, writing, astronomy and logic and brought up their sons to be warriors. Whenever a son was born a dagger was placed at his side so that he could make it a means of living.[2]

They lived on the banks of rivers--the men on one bank and women on the other. On a fixed date the women crossed over on to the men's side returning home early in the morning. Any man consorting with them on any other day was liable to have his teeth and nails pulled out and was put to death.[3]

As the Muslim power extended,more and more tribes came under subjection and the Turks came into specialnotice of the conquerors by virtue of the valour of their men and the beauty of their women.[4]

Slaves

The development of a slave institution started when the Abbasid Caliph, Al-Mutasim, on his accession in 833 AD, reduced the pay of free Arabs and then let their summons lapse, using the money saved on their pension for buying Turkish slaves. The practice was followed by provincial dynasties and, by the 11th century A.D., most middle eastern armies were built around a nucleus of slaves. They came from Greece, Armenia, China and other places but it was the Turks who were renowned for loyalty and valour. In Ghazni, the Sultan's personal bodyguard formed an elite corps within the slave hierarchy being known as *Ghulam-i-saraj; Ghulaman-i-khass* or *Ghulaman-i-Sultan.*

They had their own set of officers and received their orders not directly from the army commander but through a liaison officer. They had their own standard, bearing a lion device, and when dismounted for ceremonial purposes, had their own special arms--the short spear (*tirad, mitrad*), the bow and the mace (*gurz, amud*). They lined the Sultan's audience chamber and surrounded the monarch seated on his dais. They wore rich robes of the finest brocades from Isfahan, Baghdad and Shushtar, and their weapons were heavily bejewelled with gold and silver mountings.[5]

Some of the Turkish slaves came through conquest but others were sold into slavery by enemies of the family or even by their own kinsmen, greedy for money or jealous of the superior qualities of their relative. Many had no recollection of their origin or family and made the land they went into their own and rose to positions of prestige and power.[6]

Slowly they replaced the Persians as royal bodyguard and, through sheer force of talent and efficiency, became extremely powerful in the Abbasid Caliphate. A story illustrating their role of king maker is told about the Caliph Mutazz (866-869) who summoned an astrologer and asked him how long he would live and retain the Caliphate. The answer came glibly from a wit, "As long as the Turks please". This was greeted by loud laughter.[7]

Zurji Zayadan wrote "Where as at first the Turkish captains swore allegience to the Caliphs, presently the Caliphs swear allegiance to them." As the power of the Turks increased many of them converted to Islam and migrated towards the West.[8]

The Turks also formed the backbone of the bureaucracy and slaves were trained to fill important posts. Slave trading became one of the most profitable business ventures and traders who invested in good education and training of the slaves reaped rich harvests.[9]

The central authority in those times was seldom strong enough to enforce discipline in the provinces and governors were apt to revolt and assert their independence. In this context, loyalty and submission were the main assets of the Turkish slave. Torn from his tribe and kinsmen he had no loyalty but that to his master, whose property he was, and in royal service to whom there was honour and pride. Every sphere of his life, private or public, was under the personal control of his master. He was not free to marry according to his own choice (many masters insisted that Turks must marry Turk in order to perpetuate the qualities of loyalty and valour). He could not entertain or even visit fellow officers without his master's consent. Any property belonging to him was inherited not by his children but by the monarch who, as compensation, looked after his family and often took his sons into service. To be the slave of a king merited special respect since it could open a pathway right to the top. "The slave of today is the Sultan of tomorrow", says an old proverb.

Any status gained was strictly on the basis of merit rather than favouritism.No favour of partiality was shown and any one who rose to the top did so because of his innate talent, unremitting labour and genius for survival.[10]

Training

In the *Siyasat Namah*, Niam-ul-Mulk describes the career of a Turkish slave in the Sasanid empire (874-999)."They advanced slaves gradually, taking account of their services, their courage and their merit. Thus a slave who had just been purchased served one year on foot. Clothed in a cotton tunic he walked beside the stirrup of his chief; they did not have him mount on horseback either in public or in private and would be punished if it was learnt that he had done so. When his first year of service was ended, the head of the chamber informed the Chamberlain and the latter gave the slave a Turkish horse which had only a rope in its mouth, a bridle and halter in one. When he had served one year on horseback, whip in hand, he was given a leather girth to put on the horse. The fifth year they gave him a better saddle, a bridle ornamented with stars, a tunic of cotton mixed with silk and mace which he suspended by a ring from his saddle bow. In the sixth year he received a garment of more splendid colour and in his seventh year they gave him a tent held up by a pole and fixed with sixteen pegs; he had three slaves in his suite and he was honoured with title of a head of the Chamber; he wore on his head a hat of black felt embroidered with silver and he was clothed with a silk robe. Every year he was advanced in place and dignity, his retinue and escort were increased until the time when he reached the rank of Chief of squadron and finally that of a Chamberlain. Though his capacity and merit might be recognised, though he had done some noteworthy deed and acquired universal esteem and the affection of his sovereign, he was obliged, neverthe less, to wait until the age of 35 before obtaining the title of Amir and a government."[11]

A Turkish slave, male or female, could fetch as much as 3,000 *dinars*. Some free Turks worked as traders and artisans or sold vegetables and baked bread. Because of their pride, however, they demanded equality of treatment not being content to do menial jobs.[12]

Muizuddin Muhammad bin Sam had no sons to succeed him. He liked owning Turkish slaves and bought a great number of them. All his slaves were renowned for their bravery, expertise in administration etc. Concerned about the fate of the empire after his death, a confidante of the Sultan said to him. "To a monarch like unto thee, the like of whom in height of dignity and grandeur the whole expanse of the empire of Islam does not contain, sons were necessary to thy empire, in order that every one of them might be the inheritor of a kingdom of the empire of the universe so that, after the expiration of the period of (this) present reign the sovereignty might continue firmly in this family." To this the Sultan replied,"Other monarchs may have one son or two sons: I have so many thousand sons, namely, my Turk slaves, who will be the heirs of my dominion and who, after me, will take care to preserve my name in the Khutbah throughout those territories."[13]

Apart from Qutb-ud-Din Aibak and Shams-ud-Din Iltutmish who became kings, a host of other Turkish warriors, noted for their bravery and sagacity, helped set up and consolidate the Sultanate of Delhi. Among these may be mentioned the following three:

MUHAMMAD-I-BAKHTIYAR KHALJI

Muhammad bin Bakhtiyar of the Khalji tribe of Ghur and the territory of Garmsir, was a man of great ability--bold, impetuous,enterprising and sagacious. But when he came to the court of Muiz-ud-Din Muhammad bin Sam at Ghazni, his humble and unprepossessing appearance procured for him from the *Diwan-i-Ariz* (department of the muster master) only a small stipend. This he rejected and came to Delhi where, also, his appearance went against him and he was refused employment. In Badaun, however, he managed to find employment but only on a low level. Luck came to him when his paternal uncle, Muhammad bin Mahumud, fought in the battle of Tarain where Rae Pithora was defeated and found service with Ali Nagairi who conferred a kettle-drum and banner upon him and made him feudatory of Kashmandi. On his uncle's death, Muhammad-bin-Bakhtiyar became feudatory in his place.

After having acquired sufficient arms and having displayed bravery in many places, he went to Awadh where the fiefs of Bhagwat and Bhiwali were conferred on him. Not content with this small domain he made repeated incursions into the territory of Muner and Bihar obtaining a great deal of booty and a large number of men, a great many of them of his own tribe, in his service. All this gained him great fame and Qutb-ud-Din Aibak sent him a robe of honour.

This encouraged him in his incursions towards Bihar until he organised an attack on the fort of Bihar itself. After capturing the fort with only a very few men, with whom he had ridden ahead of his army, he found a vast library and discovered that the whole fortress was a college as the name Bihar signified in the local language.

After this victory, he returned to Delhi with great booty and received great honour and distinction from Aibak, who at that time was the representative of Sultan Muiz-ud-Din Muhammad-bin-Sam and had not yet become Sultan. All this made many of the *Amirs* jealous and, at a banquet, he was derided and jeered at and then goaded on to fight an elephant at the Kasr-i-Safed (white castle) which later became the imperial palace. One blow of the Khalji's mace on its trunk however, terrified the elephant which fled.

This brought further honours and a special robe of honour from his own wardrobe from Aibak who also commanded the *Amirs* to bestow gifts on the Khalji resulting in his receiving so many gifts "as could not be contained within the limits of writing." Muhammad-bin-Bakhtiyar kept the honorary dress but bestowed the rest of the presents on the people and set out towards Bihar.

His fame had preceded him and struck fear in the hearts of the people of Lakhnauti and Bihar and the kingdoms of Bang and *Kamrup*. It also reached Rae Lakhmaniah, ruler of the city of Nudiah, a very great man who had been ruler for eighty years.

Minhaj recounts a story about Rae Lakhmaniah. His father died before the Rae's birth. The crown was placed on his mother's belly, and since the Rae's family was regarded with great reverence by other Hindu rulers, she was well served and looked after. When the time of birth drew near, the mother called together a number of astrologers who, unanimously, informed her that if the child was born at the time when birth seemed imminent he would be extremely unfortunate and never become king. If on the other hand, the birth could be delayed by two hours he would rule for eighty years. Hearing this, the mother had herself suspended with her head downwards and feet bound together. When the auspicious hour arrived she directed that she should be taken down. The child Lakhmaniah was born and placed on the throne but the mother died.

As predicted, he reigned for eighty years, gaining renown for his generosity and helpfulness to all and for never having committed a single tyrannical act. Like Qutb-ud-Din Aibak he was known to be a bestower of lakhs in his own currency, the cowrie shell.

As at the time of his birth, the astrologers foretold his downfall at the hands of the Turks led by a man with unnaturally long-arms-the marked characteristics of Muhammad-i-Bakhtiyar's physique.

From Bihar, Muhammad-bin-Bakhtiyar Khalji pressed on to Nudiah and with a total of 18 men took the fort, the ruler having had already allowed the Brahmins and a large number of inhabitants, who apprehended danger from the approaching Turkish army, to leave the fort and he fled barefooted by the back entrance of his palace leaving dishes of gold and siliver full of food. All his treasure, wives, other women, his attendants, and servants were taken into custody. The Rae fled towards Sankanat and Bang where he died, but his desendants continued to rule for sometime.

Muhammad-i-Bakhtiyar made Lakhnauti his capital and instituted in every part of the territory the reading of the *Khutbah* and the coining of money, obviously in the name of the ruling Sultan Muiz-ud-Din Muhammad bin Sam. He sent a large part of the booty and the captured wealth to Qutb-ud-Din in Delhi.

After establishing full control over the conquered territory, Muhammad-i-Bakhtiyar's restlessness reasserted itself and he decided to take the countries of Turkestan and *Tibbat*. He was guided through the mountainous country by a man of the Mej tribe who had converted to Islam and was known as Ali the Mej. He came to the river Brahmaputra, which is described by Minhaj as being three times larger than the Ganges, and called in the Hindwi dialect Samund (ocean) Minhaj erroneously names this river the Beg-mati.

Muhammad-bin-Bakhtiyar went along the river until he reached a point where it could be spanned by a bridge and built one consisting of more than twenty arches. After crossing the bridge he received an embassy from the ruler of Kamrup advising him not to attempt to reach *Tibbat* at that time. He was told to return and make ample preparations before trying again the following year when the Rae of Kamrup promised to help him in the venture. But the obsessed Khalji refused to heed the counsel and continued in his endeavour.[14]

The boundaries of Kamrup are very loosely described by Muslim authors who apply the name to all the territory between the northern frontiers of the Bangalah territory conquered by the Muslims and the hills of Bhutan, the southern boundary being where the Lakhiyah river separates from the Bramaputra.[15]

After crossing the river the army pressed on and on the sixteenth day it reached the open country of *Tibbat*. They found the whole tract to be well cultivated with populous villages inhabited by various tribes. There was a strong fort, the inmates of which fought a fierce battle armed with spears, cuirasses, shields, helmets and body armour all made of bamboo. Minhaj says that the people of th e area were all Turks, who had probably settled there long before the conquerors took Delhi.

A number of Muhammad-bin-Bakhtiyar's troops were killed and on enquiry from some captured inmates of the fort, he learnd that messenger had been sent to the city of Kar-pattan where 50,000 Turkish horsemen and archers were available and would reach the fort the next day. He learned that the route they would take would be the *Mahanmah-i-Darah*, the terrain of which was rough and craggy with 35 passes between the territory of Tirhut and Kamrup.

His army being already fatigued by the march and the first day's fighting having taken a very heavy toll of dead and injured, Muhammad-i-Bakhtiyar, now hearing of the nature of the land, decided to retreat to make adequate preparation and return the next year to conquer the territory. On the way back, he faced disaster for the enemy had used the scorched earth technique, burning all the vegetation along the route and removing the inhabitants to other areas. Not a pound of food for the men or a blade of grass could be found for the cattle and horses and, for fifteen days on the march the men survived by killing their horses and eating them.

When they finally reached the bridge they had constructed on the river, they found that the two *Amirs* who had been left to guard it had fallen out with each other and had neglected the bridge allowing it to fall into disrepair, and had finally gone off and left it unattended. It had been destroyed by the Kamrup troops.

Thus, when Muhammad-bin-Bakhtiyar reached the place the found no way of crossing the river, boats not being available. They took refuge in a temple full of huge beautiful idols made of gold and silver. Here, on the orders of the Kamrup ruler, the local people tried to imprison them by planting spiked bamboos into the ground and weaving them together to form a strong wall. Seeing this the imprisoned troops rushed out of the temple and with considerable difficulty, Muhammad-bin-Bakhtiyar made a road for himself and his followers and reached the bank of the river.

Some of the soldiers plunged their horses into the water and finding the river fordable, urged their companions to follow them. However, in mid-stream the river turned out to be very deep and soldiers and horses all perished, with the exception of Muhammad-i-Bakhtiyar and about a hundred horsemen who managed somehow to cross the river.

Thereafter, Muhammad-bin-Bakhtiyar was helped by the relatives of Ali, the Mej (what happened to him is not mentioned) untill he reached Diwnot. The whole incident had had a very bad effect on him and he fell grievously ill, ashamed both of his defeat and the fate of the troops who had perished in the venture. Whenever he rode out in the city the relatives of the deceased, women and children, would wail from rooftops and heap abuses and accusations against him until he stopped venturing out.

During all this time he was heard constantly repeating, "Can any calamity have befallen the Sultan-i-Ghazi (Muizuddin Muhammad bin Sam) that my good fortune hath deserted me?" His guess was correct for it was at that time that Muizuddin had been assassinated. When the news reached Muhammad-bin-Bakhtiyar he took to his bed and died. According to a story an Amir of his, Ali-i-Mardan who had been given the fief of Narankoe, came to Diw-kot on hearing of the disaster and some how managed to find his way to the sick-room where Muhammad-bin-Bakhtiyar lay, and which no one had been able to enter for three days. Drawing the sheet from his face Ali killed him with a dagger. Thus, Muhammad died in the same year in which the other Muhammad, his master, died.[16]

NASIR-UD-DIN QABACHA

Another towering personality of the times was Nasir-ud-Din Qabacha. According to Raverty, the nickname Qabacha is spelt with slight variation in different manuscripts. If it is 'Qabacha' it would signify a short jacket or tunic, and would make him to be Nasir-ud-Din of the short jacket or tunic from a favoured costume. Spelt with 'Gh' with one 'b' it would signify rending, tearing, cutting etc; while if spelt 'kabba' it would signify slender waisted. Thus, the nickname could be said to mean "very slender-waisted".[17]

He was a slave of Muhammad Muiz-ud-Din bin Sam and is described by Minhaj as being endowed with great intellect, sagacity, discretion, skill, wisdom and experience, qualities which he had displayed in his many years' service in various departments and thus acquired great influence. He was made feudatory of Uchchah.

He had married two of Aibak's daughters, one after the other, and by the elder daughter had a son Malik Ala-ud-Din Bahram Shah, a handsome young man of pleasant manners but given to pleasure and vice.

After Aibak's death Bahram shah took over the territories of Multan, Siwastan and Diwal extending his kingdom upto the sea coast. He also brought under his sway the cities and fortresses of Sind, assumed two canopies of State and, in the east, annexed the territories of Tabarhindah, Kuhram and Sursu. He also occupied Lahore several times fighting the troops of Ghazni which were sent to the Punjab by Taj-ud-Din Yalduz who had installed himself on the throne of Ghazni. First he was thrown out of Lahore by the Ghazni Wazir, Mu-ayyid-ul-mulk, Muhammad-i-Abdullah, the Sanjari, and later by Yalduz himself.

There was constant friction between Qabacha and Iltutmish who had been installed as ruler of Delhi and the former was defeated by Iltutmish in 614 AH. The arrival on the banks of the Indus of Jalal-ud-Din Mankbarni, son of Khwarazm Shah, who was being chased by the Mongols, and the arrival of Chengiz Khan himself in pursuit of his quarry changed the picture. Mankbarni proceeded towards Diwal and Mukran and the Mongol chief Turti appeared at the foot of the walls of the city of Multan, having taken Nandanah, and besieged it for 42 days in 621 AH but was unable to take it.

During the siege, Qabacha spent lavishly to benefit the people and "showed such proofs of boldness, ability and courage that the mention thereof will endure upon the pages of time until the judgment day."

One and a half years later, the *Maliks* of Ghur, harassed by the Mongols, joined Qabacha. A very short while later, in the latter part of the year, 623 AH, a body of the Khalj tribe, a part of the Khwarazmi forces, acquired supremacy over the district of Mansurah, one of the cities of Siwastan, and were repelled by Qabacha. Their chief, Malik Khan, was slain.

In 624 AH, Minhaj reached the city of Uchchah by boat from Khorasan by way of Ghazni and Banian, and was made head of the Firuzi College of Uchchah and Kazi of the forces of Ala-ud-Din Bahram Shah, Qabacha's son. The same year, Iltutmish pitched his camp within sight of Uchchah. Nasir-ud-Din Qabacha perhaps fatigued by all the previous happenings, chose not to face him but retired by boat to Bhakar. He was pursued by Iltutmish's forces, led by the wazir, which besieged the fortress in which he had sought refuge.

In spite of Qabacha's departure, the fortress of Uchchah held out for two months and twenty-seven days when it surrendered to Iltutmish. Hearing of this calamity, Qabacha sent his son, Alu-ud-Din, to Iltutmish. Soon after this embassy reaching Uchchah, the fortress of Bhakar was taken. Unwilling to face humiliation and defeat, Qabacha preferred to drown himself. He had held sway over the territories of Multan, Uchchah and Sind for 22 years.[18]

TAJ-UD-DIN-YALDUZ

Taj-ud-Din Yalduz is described by Minhaj as being of excellent faith, mild, beneficent, of good disposition and very handsome. No accurate translation of the name 'Yalduz' exists. It may just have been a fanciful nickname given to him at birth, or it may have been connected with some trifling incident. He was bought by SultanMuizuddin Muhammad bin Sam while young and was, from the start, given a good position and enjoyed the Sultan's confidence and rose, at an early age, to be Chief of the other Turkish slaves. After he grew up, the Sultan made him feudatory of Sankuran and Kamran. Every year, the Sultan would stop in Kamran on his way from Ghazni on his incursions into India, and Taj-ud-Din Yalduz would hold elaborate feasts for the Sultan and his nobles presenting them with a thousand honorary head dresses and quilted tunics. The rest of the retinue would be housed and fed and given presents of money.

On his last visit to Kamran, which happened to be the last year of his life, the Sultan was presented with usual 1000 head dresses and tunics. He selected one of each and presenting Yalduz with his own royal apparel conferred on him a black banner indicating that it was his wish that Yalduz should succeed him to the throne of Ghazni.

At the Sultan's command, he married one of his daughters to Qutb-ud-Din Aibak and the other to Nasir-ud-Din Qabacha. He had two sons, one of whom he had placed under a preceptor. One day, as an act of enforcing discipline, the preceptor hit the boy on the head with an earthen water jar. The blow proved fatal and the boy died. On receiving news of the tragedy, Yalduz sent money to the preceptor with the advice "that he should get out of the way and undertake a journey, before the boy's mother became aware of her son's fate, lest she might cause any injury to be done him, in anguish for the loss of her son."

On Muizuddin's death, the Turkish nobles invited Ghiyas-ud-Din Mahmud, the son of his brother, Ghiyas-ud-Din, to come from Garmsir to Ghazni to occupy his uncle's throne and save the territory from the threat of occupation by the Sultans of Bamian. Ghiyas-ud-Din Mahmud rejected the offer saying, "I confer the territory (of Ghazni) on you." At the same time, he sent a letter of manumission and a robe of honour to Yalduz and assigned to him the throne of Ghazni.

Having received this mandate, Yalduz came to Ghazni, ousted the *Maliks* of Bamian and ascended the throne. Thereafter, twice he was ousted from Ghazni and twice he returned. Eventually, he fought a battle with Qutab-ud-Din Aibak in the Punjab and was defeated. For a third time, Yalduz advanced upon Ghazni and occupied the throne, Aibak retreating to India via the Sang-i-Surakh.

On several occasions he sent his armies towards Ghur, Herat and Sijistan and on one occasion despatched a force to aid Sultan Ghiyas-ud-Din Mahmud as far as the gates of Herat to fight the *Malik* of that city who had conspired with Muhammad Khwarazm Shah, to oust the ruler of Ghur from his throne.

There were also other rebellions and disaffections during Yalduz's absence from India; the Amirs and Maliks of Ghazni put to death the wazir, Khwaja Muayyid-ul-mulk, Muhammad-i-Abd-ullah Sanjari and the Amir-i-Shikar, Malik Nasir-ud-Din Husain who had rebelled against Yalduz. Around the same time, Muhammad Khwarazm Shah advanced on Ghazni from the direction of Tukharistan and, in an unexpected manoeuvre, seized the frontier route leading into India towards Gurdaiz and the Karahah Pass.

Yalduz, who was on his way back to Ghazni, retreated to Lahore by way of the Sang-i-Surakh (There are many passes mentioned as routes from Ghazni to Lahore. Three or four of them are named Sang-i-Surakh, 'perforated stones'.)[18] where he was attacked and defeated by Iltutmish, who was his own son-in-law and on whose ascendency to the throne of Delhi, he had conferred in his capacity of the overlord of the empire of Ghur, the insignia of sovereignty. He was taken prisoner and sent to Badaun where he was executed and a mausoleum erected in his memory. He had reigned for a period of nine years.[20] After Muizuddin's death the question of succession arose. Since he had no son there could not be any dynastic succession and his three great slave officers, Qutbuddin Aibak, Nasiruddin Qabacha and Tajuddin Yalduz refused to surrender the conquered territories over which they wielded power and his easy going nephew Nasiruddin therefore had no choice but to hand them the *Khat-i-Azadi*, letter of manumission. By this one act he set free not only the three great generals but also all other slaves since without a master there can be no slave. The slaves thus became neither the slaves nor employees of the Sultan of Delhi but his co-heirs. The Sultan, thus reduced to the status of prima inter pares, first among equals, could hold office only if he kept them all pleased. The role of king maker of the Turkish slaves thus became even more stronger in Delhi.

This was the genesis of the troubles that the early rulers of Delhi faced. The throne, though supposedly hereditary could be occupied through force and intrigue only by those of whom the strong approved.

Although Turkish slaves were required to help with the administration of the new kingdom the most important positions were held by those who had helped Muizuddin set up the kingdom of Delhi. It was a closed circle allowing no outsiders, and especially afraid of Indian Muslims from whom they apprehended maximum danger.

CHIHALGANI

The title Chihalgani, 'forty families', given to the Ghurian aristocracy was purely arbitrary. The highest echelons never reached that number and the number of officers from their ranks rose to well over a thousand. They held all the senior posts from *Vakilship* or Regency to the *Kotwalship* of forts. However, there were not enough of them to man all the posts, and some senior posts in revenue, correspondence and other departments were open to others also.

The empire in India was an accepted reality and it was regarded as a permanent entity where power and prestige were to be acquired and maintained. The Turkish governors, therefore, tried to make themselves independent or to become part of a clique that would give them enough clout at Delhi. Officers' revolts became a menace to the rulers of Delhi and could be solved only by compromise leading to promotion of transfer.

When Balban ascended the throne in 1260 he saw the annihilation of the Turkish aristocracy as the only way of strengthening the throne of Delhi. Through murder, poison and assassination he sought to curb the power of the nobles but it took thirty years for him to finally end the power of the slaves.[21]

THE MONGOLS AND TURKS

Alauddin Ata Juwayni, in the *Tarikh-i-Jahan Gusha*, has compared the military organisation of the Changizi Mongols and the Khwarizmian Turks to the detriment of the latter. "The muster and marking of the army" (of the Mughals) he says, "have been organised in such a way as to dispense with the office of Review and dismiss its officers and deputies. The whole mass of the fighting people has been divided into groups of tens, and one man out of every ten is appointed amir over the remaining nine (Amir-i-dah) Out of ten such amirs, one is named amir-i-sadah and all the100 men are placed under his command. This goes on till the (amir of) thousand (Amir-i-Hazara) and over10,000 men is placed as Amir-i-Tuman. If there is a problem to face, or men and things required, the matter is referred (by the supreme ruler) to the Amir-i-Tuman who informs the Amir-i-Hazara in his turn till the order ultimately reaches the Amir-i-dah." He continues, "Equity and justice are enforced in case one person is tormented by another and no consideration paid to outward status or position. If suddenly a force is required, it is ordered that so many thousands be present at such a time and place, and without a moment's hesitation and delay the order is carried out. The spirit of discipline and loyalty exists to such a degree that if an individual, be he the commander of a thousand, commits wrong, and in spite of a distance of east and west between him and the Khan, a rider is despatched to carry out the punishment, or to cut off his head or to exact gold as ordered. Quite unlike is the position of the ruler (of a Muslim country) who talks with fear with his own purchased slave, if the latter possesses ten horses in his State, lest some evil should result from it. If an army is placed under his command and he attains to a position of authority he simply cannot be commanded. And often it happens that the officer himself rises to revolt (against the king) and whenever the king wishes to attack an enemy or an enemy wishes to attack him, they take months and years to put the army in order and treasuries and territories are required for their salaries and pay. On traditional and ceremonious occasions, they are present by hundreds and thousands, but at the time of war and death struggle the lines are broken and none turns up on the battlefield. There is a parable which holds particularly true of their organisation. At the time of realising taxes a revenue officer demanded a number of goats from a farmer. The farmer said "wherefrom"? The oficer answered "In the records". The farmer continued "Yes, but there is none in the flock." The same is true of Muslim troops. The Amir shows that he has such a number of men under him in order to receive more than legitimate pay, but on the occasion of review they practice deceit so as to make up the total.''[22]

''The Turks'', writes Md.Habib, ''were educated, brave, liberal, patrons of art and learning, courteous in social contacts, cordial and humorous with an urbanity of manners borrowed from Persia. They spent money lavishly, some of it borrowed from Hindu bankers. They drank profusely, prayed and fasted regularly and patronised mullahs and nautch girls with an equal hand. They were patrons of all the arts--architecture, astrology, geomancy (ramal), hunting, education, scholarship and mural painting (no example of which unfortunately remains). But they were aggressive, self-assertive and tyrannical striking brutally at all who crossed them whether in battle or on the street. They formed a marked contrast to the Indian Muslim and the Indian at large, who was himself mild and retiring by temperament, and struck horror in their hearts so that even the Muslim tried to keep out of their way and not to enter their services except in case of dire necessity.''

He describes them thus, ''Short in stature but with a frame of steel that could stand both the strain of war and the orgies of drunkenness, with a red face, red or flaxen hair, a sparse moustache and a pointed beard of limited dimensions the central Asian Turk was an odd, in fact, a hideous figure on the Indian landscape where people always preferred a retiring and mild character. He appeared self-assertive, presumptuous, brutal and tyrannical. In the social gathering of Indian Muslims, his presence was never welcome and no one wept at the fate that finally overtook him.''[23]

Their shortcomings, however, were no hindrance to their gaining spectacular victories. Between 1191 and 1205, the Turkish rule spread to Punjab, Sindh, Oudh, Bihar, Bengal and parts of Rajasthan and Gujarat. Without any special aids to conquest, such as artillery or navy or special weapons, the Turks maintained an amazing pace of conquest and consolidation and set up the capital, Delhi, that remained the centre of an empire (although ruled by different dynasties and with fluctuating fortunes) until 1857.

Notes

1. Fakhruddin Mubarak Shah, *Tarikh-i-Mubarak Shah*, ed. by E.D. Ross, p. 38. Hereinafter referred to as Mubarak Shah.
2. Ibid., p. 42.

3. Ibid., p. 40-41.
4. Ibid., p. 35.
5. C.E. Bosworth, *The Ghaznavids, their Empire in Afghanistan and Eastern Iran*, p. 90. Hereinafter referred to as Bosworth.
6. Mubarak Shah, p. 35.
7. Muhammad Aziz Ahmad, *Political History and Institutions of the Early Turkish Empire in India*, p. 4. Hereinafter referred to as Muhammad Aziz Ahmad.
8. Elliot & Dowson, *History of India as Told by its Own Historians*, Vol. II, Foreword by Md. Habib, p. 92.
9. Muhammad Aziz Ahmad, p. 4.
10. Ibid., pp. 5-6.
11. Nizam ul Mulk Tusi, *Syasat-Namah*, p. 75.
12. Bosworth, p. 11.
13. Minhaj-us-Siraj, *Tabaqat-i-Nasiri*, p. 497, Hereinafter referred to as Minhaj.
14. Ibid., pp. 548-561.
15. Minhaj-us-Siraj, *Tabaqat-i-Nasiri*, edited and translated by Major H.G. Raverty, p. 561, footnote 3. Hereinafetr referred to as Raverty.
16. Minhaj, pp. 562-573.
17. Raverty, p. 531 footnote 8.
18. Minhaj, pp. 531-544.
19. Minhaj, pp. 496-506.
20. Raverty, p. 505 footnote 6.
21. Md. Habib, *Politics and Society during Early Medieval Period*, pp. 105-107. Hereinfater referred to as Habib.
22. Muhammad Aziz Ahmad, pp. 40-41.
23. Habib, pp. 108-109.

GLOSSARY

Abbasids	The third line of the Caliphs who ruled the Islamic East from Baghdad
Abdariya	River water
Adab-ul-Harb	Techniques of warfare, part of the title of Fakhr Mudabbir's famous 13th century treatise: *Adab-al-Harb-wa-al-Shujaat*
Adls	Coins of copper
Ahkam	Plural of hukm, commandments, orders
Ahl-i-Qalam	Men of literature
Ahl-i-Saif	Men of sword
Akhurbeg	Supdt. of royal horses
Alim	A theologian, plural Ulema
Amils	Revenue officers
Amir-ash-Shura	Chief of the poets, the Court poet, poet laureate.
Amir-i-Akhur	Minister-in-charge of stables
Amir-i-Hajib	Minister of the court incharge of ceremonies
Amir-i-kuh	Officer-in-charge of agriculture
Amir-i-Mutribin	Chief of the musicians, the Court musician
Amir-i-Shikar	Incharge of royal hunt

Amirs	Noblemen
Arbab	People at the helm of affairs
Arid, Ariz, Arid-i-Mamalik, Ariz-i-Mamalik	Officer-in-charge of the muster, equipment of the soldiers and their horses
Ashura	The tenth day of the first lunar month Muharram, the day of the martyrdom of Imam Husain
Awaz-i-Khalq	Voice of the people, public opinion
Awqaf	Plural of waqf, endowments, bequests for pious and charitable purposes
Bad mazhaban	Plural of *bad mazhab*, a heretic, an idolator
Bait-ul-Mal	Money belonging to the state treasury
Barbek	Officer-in-charge of the royal court
Barid	Intelligence officer
Barid-i-Mumalik	Head of state news agency
Barshkal	Rain, rainy season
Bazar	A market place
Bazar-i-Bazazan	Cloth merchants' bazar
Bhakti	Devotion
Bhand	Bard, mimic, balladeer
Bigha	A unit of measurement of land
Billion Jital	Coins of silver and bronze alloy
Bimaristan	Hospital

Bira	Folded betel with ingredients
Brahman	Highest caste of Hindus
Chihalgani	The group of forty nobles constituted by Sultan Iltutmish
Chandala	A lowly placed, non-descript, untouchable caste
Chashnigir	A taster to a prince, royal cup bearer
Chatr, Chhattri	Royal umbrella
Chaudhuris	A class of village headmen
Chaugan	The medieval polo
Dabir	Registrar/record keeper
Dabir-i-Khas	Special scribe - repository of state secrets
Dabri-i-Sara	Registrar of the palace
Dailamis	A dynasty in power in Persia
Dak chauki	Postal station
Dalan	Courtyard of a mansion
Damishmand	Wise man
Dana	The wise
Dandas	Sticks/punishment
Dang	A small coin, the fourth part of a dirham

Dar-ul-Aman	Land of peace, an ally's territory, a division of the world according to the Islamic law, the other two divisions are Dar-ul-Islam (land of Islam) and Dar-ul-Harb (enemy's territory), land of war; also name of a part of Delhi which contained the sepulchres (now in ruins), of Balban and his son Prince Muhammad
Dar-ul-Shafa	Hospital and health centre
Dar-us-Sultanat	The capital of the Sultanate
Dargah	The court, mausoleum of a saint, shrine
Darwesh	Saints/mendicants
Dastar	The turban
Deva Davia	Qualities of the gods
Dawah	Claim
Dawatdar	Keeper of the inkpot
Delhiwala or Delhiwal	Coins of mixed metal
Devi	Deity
Dinars	Roman silver coins
Dirham	Roman copper coin
Diwan	Minister
Diwan-i-Amir-i-koh	Office of the *Amir-i-kuh*
Diwan-i-ard	Office of the Ministry of War
Diwan-i-Isha	Office of the chief secretary, the royal chancellery

Diwan-i-Mazalim	Court of crime
Diwan-i-Qada	Court of faith
Diwan-i-Qaza	Office of the chief Qazi
Diwan-i-Risalat	Office of the Secretary of Foreign and Diplomatic relations
Diwan-i-wizarat	Office of the Wazir
Do-aspah	A soldier with two horses, a post boy
Doaba	Land between the Ganga and the Yamuna
Durbar	Holding court with noblemen
Durbash	Sash
Fal	Omen
Faraiz	Duties
Farrash	A menial servant
Farsakh	A measure of distance, about two miles
Fatawa	Eches
Fatehnama	Letter or message of victory
Fatimids	A dynasty in power in Egypt, with claim to Caliphate
Fidais	Persons devoted absolutely to any cause, Ismailis
Fiqh	Islamic jurisprudence
Futuh	Gifts and presents to a saint

Gaz	Yard
Ghazals	Special poetry rendering in Urdu
Ghulam	Slaves
Ghulam-i-Saraj	Common slaves
Ghulaman-i-Sultan	Slaves of the Sultan
Ghulaman-i-khas	Special slaves, royal slaves
Gimarbazi	Gambling
Gurbeg	Keeper of the arsenal
Guru	Religious head, preceptor
Gurz	Mace
Hadia	Gift, present
Haqiqat	Reality-truth
Hadises, Hadiths	Words, sayings or acts of the Prophet
Hajib	Senior soldiers (captain)
Halwa	A kind of sweetmeat
Hamam	Bath
Hanafites	Sect in Islam
Hashia	Margin, frill, footnote
Hulya	Appearance, bearing or quality of a person
Ihtiker	Regrating, cornering

Ilm-i-faraiz	Knowledge of duties
Imam	Highest dignitary to interpret Islamic laws
Imarat-i-ammah	Ordinary governors
Imarat-i-khassah	Special governors
Iqta	Revenue assignment
Iqtadar	Holder of an iqta, governor
Jagirs	Assignment of the revenue of a tract of land by the State to its officers by way of payment of their salaries
Jamaat-khana	A Chisti hospice
Jandars	Bodyguards
Jihad	Holy war against infidels enjoined upon the Muslims
Jital	Coin of the realm
Jizya	Has two meanings—(a) in the literature of the Delhi Sultanate; any tax which is not *Kharaj* or land tax, (b) in the *Shariat*, a personal and yearly tax on non-Muslims
Kaba	Sanctotum of the holy mosque at Mecca
Kafir	Infidel
Kalimah	The Muslim oath of affirmation: "There is no God but Allah and Muhammad is His Messenger"
Karkhanas	Workshops

Kasr-i-Safed	the white palace of Sultan Iltutmish
Kazi	Law giver
Khalifa	Caliph, spiritual successor of a saint
khalq	The people in general, mankind
Khanqaha	Hospice
Khans	Title of noblemen(graded)
Kharaj	Land revenue, tribute paid by a subordinate ruler
Kharaji	Land from which *kharaj* is levied
Kharif	The winter crop in India
Khasab-dar	Bearer of Sultans special armour and personal arms
khat-i-azadi	The manumission letter
Khatib	person who delivers sermons after the congregational prayers
Khatib	Scribe
Khawaja	Title of Wazir at Gazni
Khazindar	Keeper of the privy purse
Khilafat	Caliphate, commandership of the faithful, succession
Khilafatnama	Letter/document of succession to the *Khalifa* from his spiritual master (pir)
Khutba	Sermon after prayer

Kitabdar	A librarian
Kos	A measure of distance, about two miles
Kotwal	Officer-in-charge of a city or a fort
Kshatriyas	The warrior and the ruler class, one of the four Hindu varnas
Kubbah or Qubbah	A dome, a cupola
Kushak-i-Firuzi	The Tarquoise palace of Sultan Iltutmish
Kushti	Wrestling
Madaniyat	Urbanity, urbanization
Madarasahs	Religious schools and colleges
Madinas	Towns, cities
Maisara	The left side, left wing of an army
Maimana	The right side, right wing of an army
Majlis	Congregation
Majlis-i-Am	Consultative council of citizens
Majlis-i-Rai	A meeting for consultations
Mal-i-Haq	Rightful goods (property or money)
Malahidah	Plural of *mulhid*, heretics, nonbelievers
Malik	Title of noble men (graded)
Malik-i- hukama	Chief physician
Malik-ut-tajir	Leaders in commerce/trade

Malikah	Queen
Maqbara	A grave, mausoleum
Mashaldar	Torch bearer and in-charge of furniture
Masjid	A mosque
Mazalim court or Diwan-i-Mazalim	Chief city magistrate
Mehta	A Hindi term for a medieval officer whose status varied in different parts of India
Minar	A tower, spire, a minaret
Miskals	Measure for precious ornaments, also coins
Mlechhas	Hindus below the four varnas, chandalas
Muftis	Ascetic religious figure
Muharram	First lunar month
Muhtab	An officer appointed to maintain law and order
Muhtasib	Guardian of public decency
Mujtahid	Interpreter of Islamic law and theology
Mullah	Priest — conversant with the Holy Quran
Mumin	A Muslim believer
Munjaniq	A catapult to shoot stone missiles
Muqaddam	A village headman
Muqaddama	First chapter or section of a book, advanced guard

Muqti	The *iqta* holder
Murji	Procastinators
Murshid	Pir, spiritual guide
Mushrif-i-Mamlakat	Custodian of all royal moveables and immovables
Mushrif-i-Mumalik	Accountant General
Mushriks	Idolators
Mustauf-i-Mumalik	Auditor General
Mutassarif	Accountant
Mutawalli	an administrator of a religious and charitable foundation
Muzakkir	One who delivers sermons
Nadims	Companions of the Sultan
Naib	Deputy
Naib Wazir	Deputy minister
Naib-Barbek	Deputy master of ceremonies
Naqib-ul-muqaba	Chief usher
Naqibs	Ushers
Nasibi	Setters up
Naubat	Beating of the drum before the residence of the king or high officers
Nauroz	New year's day according to the Persian calendar

Niyabat-i-Khudawani	Viceroy of god
Nizam-ul-Mulk	A title of the Wazir, recruited from the writer class (*ahl-i-qalam*)
Pabos	Kissing the feet
Pahalwans	Wrestlers
Paigahs	Horse breeding department
Pan	betel leaves
Payaks	footmen
Prajapati	Leader (king) of people (his subjects)
Pundits	Learned Hindus
Purdah	Curtain, also the principle of the seclusion of women
Qalb	The centre of any army, heart
Qassab	The butcher
Qazi	Justice of the Islamic court
Qazi-i-Lashkar	The qazi or the judge for the army
Qazi-i-Mumalik	Chief Justice of Islamic court
Rabi-ul-awwal	Month of the Muslim calendar
Ragas	Measure of Indian music
Rai	A Hindu chief, usually one having his own territory and army
Rais-i-Bazar	Officer-in-charge of a market, to supervise and enforce market rules and regulations

Rajab	Month of the Muslim calendar
Ramzan	The nineth lunar month, month of fasting for devout Muslims
Rana	A grade of Hindu chiefs
Ratibis	Providing food for men and animals
Rattan Work	Wicker-work
Ratti	Measure (very small) to weigh precious metal
Rawafiz	The Shias
Rawats	Title by which many Hindu chiefs were known
Rizq-i-Mauzun	Proper livelihood
Rubab	A four-stringed instrument in the form of a short-necked guitar with a surface of parchment instead of wood
Sadr	Chief
Sadr-i-Jahan	Chief Sadr of the dominion
Sadr-i-jandar	Chief of royal guards
Sadr-us-Sudur	Chief—like Chief Justice
Sahus	Merchants, money-lenders
Sahib-i-barid-i-Lashkar	Official army news writer
Saiyids	Direct descendants of the Prophet
Salar-i-Jahan	A title of high officer, lit. chief of the world
Sama	An audition party of the mystics

Samantas	The local and regional chiefs
Saqi-i-khas	Liquor server to the Sultan
Sar-silahdar	Chief of the bodyguards
Sar-chatradar	Chief bearer of the royal umbrella
Sar-Jandar	Chief of the bodyguards
Sarais	Inns
Sawar	A horseman, a trooper
Shaba'n	Name of the month in Muslim calendar
Shafites	Followers of the school of Imam Shafi in jurisprudence
Shahnah-i-fil	Superintendent of the elephant stable
Shahr	City
Shahs	Kings
Shaikh-ul-Islam	A title of high ecclesiastical officer, lit. chief of Islam
Sharabkhana	Wine cellars
Sharbat	Sweet drinks
Shariah	Islamic code/law
Shariat	Muslim law
Shatranj	Chess
Sheikh	A chief, a distinguished man, a spiritual leader

Shias	Sect of Islam: followers of Ali/Hussain
Shir-i-Murgh	Essence of chicken
Shushtari	Special kind of brocade
Sikka	Coins
Silahdar	Body gaurds of Sultan
Silsilah	Religious order
Sipahsalar	Commander
Sipahsalar-i-Hinduyan	The commander of the Hindu troopers
Sitar	Indian musical instrument
Siyasat	Politics, punishment
Sudra	One of the four Hindu varnas
Sufis	Muslim mystics
Sunnah	Tradition of the Prophet.
Sunni	Sect of Islam: who follow Sunnah
Tafsir	Explanation and interpretation of the Quran, lit. expanding and discovering the meaning of a difficult word or passage
Taj-ul-Masathir	Title of the 13th book by Hasan Nizami
Tajir	A trader
Takbir	Proclaiming the greatness of god by saying Allah-o-Akbar = God is great
Tamaddun	Culture, civilization

Tankhas	Coins of various denomination (in silver and gold)
Taraz	Name of ruler embroidered on cloth
Tasawwuf	Islamic mysticism
Tashdar	Ewer bearer
Tashrii	According to the *Shariat*
Thakurs	Kshatriyas, Hindu chiefs
Ulema	Learned men
Umara	Plural of *amir*, chiefs, nobles
Ushr	One-tenth, a tax on land owned by a Muslim in Islamic state
Ushri	The land on which *Ushr* is levied
Vakil	Agent, deputy
Vaisya	One of the four Hindu varnas
Wakil-i-dar	Controller of establishment
Wali	Governor
Wazir	Minister
Wilayat	Governorship, territory
Wizarat	The office of the *Wazir*
Zabita	A secular rule and law made by the State
Zakat	Gift or charity
Zamin	Ground, land

Zaminbos	Kissing the ground
Zi-kada	The eleventh lunar month
Zil-i-Hajib	Learned person
Zil-i-Subhani	Shadow of god
Zimmi	Protected people

BIBLIOGRAPHY

Afif, Shams-i-Siraj: "Tarikh-i-Firoz Shahi" in Elliot & Dowson, *History of India as Told by its Own Historians.* Vol. 3.

Agrawal V.S. "A Unique Treatise on Medieval Indian Coins" in *Ghulam Yazdani CommemorationVolume*, ed. H.K. Sherwani, Hyderabad, 1966.

Ahmad, Muhammad Aziz: *Political History and Institutions of the early Turkish Empire of Delhi*, Lahore, 1949.

Ahmed, M.G. Zubaid: *The Contribution of India to Arabic Literature.* Allahabad, 1946.

Al-Badaoni: *Muntakhabu-t-Tawarikh* by Abdul Qadir Ibn-i-Muluk Shah known as Al-Badaoni Vol. I, tr. & ed. by George S.A. Ranking, Reprint. Delhi, 1973.

Alberuni: *Alberuni's India, an account of the religion, philosophy, literature, chronology, astronomy, customs, laws and astrology of India about A.D. 1030.* ed. with notes and indices by Dr. Edward C. Sachau. Reprint. Delhi, 1961.

Altekar, A.S: *The State and Government in Ancient India.* Benaras, 1949.

Al-Umari, Shihab-al-Din: *Masalik al absar fi-mamalik al-amsar: A Fourteenth Century Arab account of India under Sultan Muhammad bin Tughlaq* . Translated by Iqtidar Husain Siddiqi & Qazi Mohammad Ahmad. Aligarh, 1971.

Ali, Syed Ameer: *The Spirit of Islam.* London, 1931.

------: *A Short History of the Saracens*, London, 1927.

Arberry, A.J : *Sufism.* London, 1956.

Baihaqi, Abul Fazal: *Tarikh-i-Baihaqi,* also known as *Tarikh-e-al-i-Subuktagin.* ed. W.H. Morley. Calcutta, 1862.

Baillie, E.B: *Digest of Mohammedan Law*, London, 1875.

Berthold, W: *Turkestan Down to the Mongol Invasion.* E.J.W. Gibb Memorial Trust, 4th ed. Norfolk, 1977.

Biswas, Atreyi: *The Political History of the Hunas in India.* New Delhi, 1973.

Bosworth, C.E: *The Ghaznavids; Their Empire in Afghanistan and Eastern Iran 994-1040*. Edinburgh, 1963.

------*The Later Ghaznavids: Splendour and Decay*. Edinburgh, 1977.

Burt, Thomas Seymour: *Account of a Voyage to India* , 2 Vols. Allahabad, 1847.

Bzent, Peter: *The Mongol Emperor Genghis Khan: His Triumph and His Legacy*; 1st Edition 1976, Weidenfield & Nicolson, London.

Carr, Stephan: *Archaeology and Monumental Remains of Delhi*. Civil & Military Gazette. Delhi, 1876.

Chand, Tara: *Influence of Islam on Indian Culture*. Allahabad, 1946.

Cummings, C.F. Gordon: *In the Himalayas and on the Indian Plains*. London, 1884.

Datta, K: *Medieval India; a Miscellany,* Vols. I. to IV. Centre of Advanced Study, Dept. of History, Aligarh Muslim University. Bombay, 1970-77.

Donnet, Daniel C: *Conversion and the Poll Tax in Early Islam*. Harvard University Press, 1950.

Dutt, R.C: *Later Hindu Civilisation*. Calcutta, 1909.

Edwards, Michael: *Every Day Life in Early India*. London, 1969.

Elliot & Dowson: *History of India as Told by its Own Historians,* Vols. 1-3. London, 1867-77. Reprinted with an introduction by M. Habib and a supplement by K.A. Nizami, Allahabad, 1952.

Epigraphica Indo-Moslemica.

Ferishta, Mohamed Kasim: *History of the Rise of the Muhammedan Power in India till the year A.D. 1612*. Tr. from the original Persian of Mohamed Kasim Ferishta by John Briggs. Vol. I. Reprint. Calcutta 1966.

Fakhruddin Mubarak Shah (known as Fakhre Mudabbir): *Tarikh-i-Mubark Shah*. ed. by E.D. Ross. London, 1927.

------: *Adabul Harb wa Shuja' at*.

Fawaid ul Fuad: *Conversations of Shaikh Nasir-ud-Din Auliya*, compiled by Amir Hasan Ali Sijzi. Lucknow, 302 A.H.

------: *Conversations of Sheikh Nizamuddin of Delhi*, Recorded (130-22 by Amir Hasan Sijzi ed. Latif Malik, Lahore, 1966.

Ghoshal, U.N: *The Agrarian System in Ancient India*. Calcutta, 1930.

Gascoigo, Bamber: *The Great Mughuls*. London, 1971

Habib, Irfan : "Technological Changes and Society in 13th & 14th Centuries" Presidential address Section II. *P I H C,* Varanasi Session 1969.

Habib, M: *Hazrat Amir Khusrau*, Bombay, 1930.

------*Politics and Society during the early Medieval Period: Collected Works of Prof. Mohammad Habib*, ed. by K.A. Nizami. N. Delhi, 1974.

------& K.A. Nizami: *A Comprehensive History of India.* 12 Vols. Vol. 5, *The Delhi Sultanate (A.D. 1206-1526).* Delhi, 1970.

------& Afsar Umar Salim Khan: *The Political Theory of the Delhi Sultanate (including translation of Ziauddin Barani's Fatawa-i-Jahandari, Circa 1358-9 A.D.).* Allahabad.

Habibullah, A.M :*The Foundation of Muslim Rule in India.* Allahabad, 3 revised edition. 1976.

Hamilton, C: *The Hedaya.* Lahore, 1975.

Hanfee, Abdul Aziz: "Ameeq" in *The Historian in Khusrau*, Amir Khusrau Memorial Volume, New Delhi. Publications Division, 1975.

Havell, E.B: *Indian Architecture.* London.

Howorth, Henry: *History of the Mongols*, 3 Vols. London, 1927.

Ibn Batuta: *The Rehla of Ibn Batuta,* tr. by A. Mohd. Husain. Baroda, 1953.

------ : *Travels in Asia and Africa (1325-1354).* London, 1929.

Isami (pen name): *Futuh-us-Salatin.* ed. A.M. Husain. Agra, 1938.

Jaiswal, K.P: *Hindu Polity.* Calcutta, 1924.

Kai Kaus b. Iskandar: *Qabus-nama.* Tr. by R. Levy. London, 1951.

Kaul, H.K: *Historic Delhi: an Anthology.* Delhi, 1985.

Kautilya: *Arthasastra* Tr. by R. Shamasastry. Mysore, 1961.

Khair-ul-Majalis: *Conversations of Shaikh Nasir-ud-Din Chirag of Delhi*, complied by Hamid Qalandar. Text edited by K.A. Nizami.

Khan, Syed Ahmed: *Asar-us-Sanadid.* Kanpur, 1904

Khusrau, Shirin: *Amir Khusrau.* Text edited by Haji Ali Ahmad Khan. Aligarh, 1927.

Lane-Poole, Stanley: *Medieval India under the Mohammedan Rule.* Reprint. Delhi, 1980.

Law, N.N: *Promotion of Learning in India during Muhammadan Rule by Muhammadans.* London, 1916.

Levy, R: *The Social Structure of Islam.* Cambridge, 1957.

Lowiak, N.W: "The Horseman Type of Bengal: The Question of Commemorative issues", in *Journal of the Numismatic Society of India*, 1973.

Marco Polo (1298), *Travels*, Tr/ed. Milton Ruggoff, New York, 1961.

Majumdar, B.K: *The Military System of Ancient India.* Calcutta, 1955.

Majumdar & Pusalkar: ed. *History and Culture of the People of India* Vol. 5, *The Struggle for Empire.* 1957.

Majumdar, R.C., Raychaudhuri, H.C., Datta, K: *An Advanced History of India,* 2nd ed. London, 1950.

Manu: *Dharmashastra.* Eng. tr. " The Laws of Manu" by G. Buhler. Oxford, 1886.

Minhaj-us-Siraj Jurjani: *Tabaqat-i-Nasiri: a General History of Muha-mmedan Dynasties of Asia including Hindustan from AH 194 (810 AD) to AH 658 (1260 AD).* Tr. from the original Persian manuscripts by Major H.G. Raverty, 2 Vols. Reprint. New Delhi, 1970.

Mirza, M.W: *Life and Works of Amir Khusrau,* Punjab University, 1935.

Moreland, W.H: *The Agrarian System of Moslem India.* Cambridge, 1929.

Nazim, M: *The Life and Times of Mahmud of Ghazna.* Cambridge, 1931.

Nizami, Hasan (1217) *Tajul Maasir.* Tr. Elliot & Dowson, Vol. 2.

Nizami, K.A: *The Life and Times of Shaikh Fariduddin Ganj-i-Shakar.* Aligarh, 1955.

------ : *Salatin-i-Delhi,* K.C. Mazhabi Rujhanal. Delhi, 1968.

------ : *Some Aspects of Religion and Politics in India during the Thirteenth Century.* Delhi, 1961.

------: *Studies in Medieval Indian History.* Aligarh, 1956.

Prasad,Beni: *The State in Ancient India.* Allahabad, 1928.

Prasad, Ishwari: *Medieval India.*

Qureshi, I.H: *Administration of the Sultanate of Delhi.* 4th ed. Karachi, 1958.

Ray, H.C: *Dynastic History of Northern India,* 3 Vols. Calcutta, 1931-35.

Ray Chaudhuri, T. & Habib, I :*The Cambridge Economic History of India,* Vol. I. c.1200-1750, Cambridge, 1982.

Salim, Ghulam Husain: *Riyaz-us-Salatin (a History of Bengal)* tr. Abdus Samad. Reprint. Delhi, 1975.

Sanders, J.J: *The History of the Mongol Conquest.* London, 1971.

Shahab, Sarmadee: *Amir Khusrau's own writings about music, in Life, Times and Works of Amir Khusrau Dehlavi.* New Delhi, National Amir Khusrau Society, 1975.

Sircar, D.C. *Indian Epigraphy.* Calcutta, 1965.

Siyar-ul-Awliya. *Saiyyid Muhammad b. Mubarak Kirmani Known as Amir or Mir Khurd.* Delhi, 1302 A.H.

Sleeman, W.H: *Rambles and Recollections of an Indian Official.* 2 Vols. London, 1844.

Smith, V.A: *Early History of India.* Oxford.

Srivastava, A.L: *The Sultanate of Delhi (including the Arab Invasion of Sind)* 711-1526 AD. 2nd. ed. Agra, 1953.

Titus, Murray: *Indian Islam*. Oxford University Press, 1920.

Thomas, E.W: *Mutual Influences of Mohammedans and Hindus in India*. Cambridge, 1930.

Tod, James: *Annals and Antiquities of Rajasthan*, ed. by Willam Crooke. London, 1920.

Tripathi, R.P: *Some Aspects of Muslim Administration*. Allahabad, 1935.

Tusi, Nizam-ul-Mulk: *Siyasat Namah*. edited by M. Qazwini & M.M. Chahardihi.Tr. by H. Darke. London, 1960.

Vaidya, C.V: *History of Medieval India*. Bombay.

Wright, H. Nelson: *Catalogue of the Coins in the Indian Museum*. Vol.II.

Yezdi, Shar Fuddin Ali: *Zafarnama*. Calcutta, 1988.

Wassaf, Shiabuddin Abdullah (1328): *Tarikh-i-Wassaf*. 5 Vols. Bombay, AH 1269/1853.

INDEX